Serving God? Serving Mammon?

Stephen Green

G000240813

Marshall Pickering

An Imprint of HarperCollins*Publishers*

Marshall Pickering is an Imprint of
HarperCollins*Religious*
Part of HarperCollins*Publishers*
77–85 Fulham Palace Road, London W6 8JB

First published in Great Britain
in 1996 by Marshall Pickering

1 3 5 7 9 10 8 6 4 2

The author has consulted the NRSV Bible for the
Bible references used throughout this publication.

A catalogue record for this book is
available from the British Library

ISBN 0 551 02982 X

Printed and bound in Great Britain by
Caledonian International Book Manufacturing Ltd, Glasgow, G64

Contents

Acknowledgements

John Aldis and Jeremy Yates-Round first put the idea into my head of writing about Christian faith and the world of my work. My wife, Jay, encouraged me to do it, and provided all the support I could have wanted. In addition, several others provided invaluable assistance as this book gradually took shape. In particular, I owe thanks to a group of people – some in full-time church roles, others who work in the thick of the financial world – who devoted considerable time out of busy lives to commenting on drafts and providing constructive guidance: Lawrence Mortimer, Lesley Perry, Andrew Purkis, Andrew Radford, Max and Judith Robinson, Christopher Smallwood. In various ways, all helped me to crystallize the book. The end result is of course my responsibility, but I know that it is materially better for their help.

Introduction

Another financial crisis in the headlines: Dealers in the news – young, with ties at half-mast, shirt sleeves rolled half-way up to the elbow, and excitement and panic in their whole body language – surrounded by screens and telephones and shouting out numbers that mean nothing to the average television viewer. Then the camera turns to the dealing room economist to hear the reasons for the latest currency crisis: all due to uncompetitive exports, or to the fecklessness of government, or to the spendthrift consumer. Whatever it is, the market pronounces its judgement in a frenzy of selling.

Or the news might be of an insider trading scandal. Or stories of mismanaged or misappropriated pension funds. Or of derivatives traders racking up huge losses and concealing them in fictitious accounts. Why is all this going on? The figures seem unreal; the activities seem like nothing more than reckless gambling. Then some financial institution fails. Days of headlines follow about the threat to pensioners' incomes and to the jobs of ordinary office workers with their mortgages to pay and their families to support. Several weekends of fury follow in the Sunday newspapers: Who knew what? What was the government doing? How can financial markets which behave like casinos be brought to order?

One way or another, the financial markets have a dreadful reputation with the public. In their minds there are countless images of slick dealers gambling recklessly with depositors' money; of financial advisers promising the earth; of banks pulling the rug out from under small businesses – and then paying those City slickers with their Porsches huge bonuses for selling the currency short.

These scenarios raise several questions for Christians: Is this a corner of the kingdom of God? Should Christians have anything to do with it? Can a Christian be called to work in it? Or is it nothing but a temple of Mammon – to be avoided and denounced as the unacceptably greedy and materialistic face of capitalism? This book is not a financial textbook, nor is it a sermon about the evils of money. Instead, it aims to look at life in the markets with the perspective of Christian faith – but *from the inside*. Too often the Christian Church has spoken out against money and the markets from the outside. But we can never see the kingdom of God properly from a distance. Jesus reminds us that only when we are in the midst of it all can we find the kingdom which is in our midst. So the aim is to find the answers from within. Christians who work in the markets – are they serving God? Or are they fooling themselves and serving Mammon instead?

1

The Global Bazaar

London today is one of the main centres of a vast global financial market, a market which occupies large numbers of people (no one knows quite how many, but certainly over a million worldwide). It is a market which works round the clock and rarely, if ever, takes a break – even on Sundays, the market is open somewhere in the world. A market which links Asian cities such as Tokyo and Hong Kong with European centres such as London, Frankfurt and Paris, and with the American markets in New York and Chicago – all talking to each other in an uninterrupted chain of global trading. It is as if the Tower of Babel had been stretched horizontally round the world.

In the City of London alone there are almost 500 banks and many other companies, large and small; some well known, others obscure – stockbrokers, bullion dealers, discount houses, fund managers. Some are brash and noisy like barrow boys at a fruit and vegetable market, others are discreet and secretive. Some are aristocratic establishments with ancient pedigrees and paintings of bygone partners hanging on their boardroom walls. Others are relative newcomers: buccaneering investment houses from New York's Wall Street with very little concern for the traditional niceties of the City, or small banks with unfamiliar names from little-known countries, diffidently waving the flag.

They come from all corners of the world, and all for one purpose – to haggle and deal in the markets. On streets with medieval names which recall a long-lost past when there was a church on every corner – Fenchurch Street, Abchurch Lane, St Mary Axe and Great St Thomas Apostle – there are now banks with names like Bank Melli Iran, Sumitomo Bank and the Oversea-Chinese Banking Corporation. All of them are there to trade in the markets – to buy and sell money, foreign exchange, bonds, shares, bullion. A far cry from medieval London, where people sold the more basic necessities of life in streets with give-away names like Milk Street, Bread Street and Pudding Lane.

The City of London has a resident population of about 5,000 – and a daytime population of over a quarter of a million. They stream in from very early in the morning in cars, on motorbikes, in buses, but above all in packed commuter trains which trundle in from Essex, Kent, Surrey, Hertfordshire and further afield. The average journey time each way is probably at least an hour. Some commute from as far as Southampton, Peterborough, Dover and Bath – journeys of over two hours each way are not uncommon. If we think of the City markets as an industry or business, then they are one of the largest employers in the British economy. The number of City workers has shrunk a little over the years, as computerization has reduced the number of purely clerical roles. In the early 1970s the City was estimated to employ over 300,000. But the loss of clerical jobs has been heavily offset by growth in the number of traders of all types. Foreign exchange traders, bullion dealers, futures brokers: these used to be found in handfuls, now they are everywhere – spilling out of the pubs and bars onto the pavements at lunchtime and in the evenings.

The growth in business that all these traders represent has taken place despite (or perhaps because of) drastic changes in the City's environment. Today's City is a hard working place where many people are at their desks well before eight o'clock and are still there ten or twelve hours later. Today's City workers owe their jobs to proven professional or technical skills, and accents no longer determine promotion prospects. Gone are the days when sons of the upper classes became 'something in the City' if they knew the right contacts, had been to the right school and had not got too good a degree at university. The old social and class barriers are mostly crumbling away. Gone too are the days when the City functioned like a cosy club where stockbrokers and others made easy money in a protected and structured market – when it was possible to get away with arriving at work at a gentlemanly hour and when the legendary City lunch stretched over two hours or more and was not complete without good wine and a brandy or port to round it off. (What on earth did they manage to do in the afternoons?) There are no more armies of Bob Cratchits, who did not have long lunches and who kept the books in big manual ledgers; or top-hatted gentlemen from the discount houses calling on the banks to collect their surplus bills for discounting; or uniformed messengers who tramped the streets carrying bills and cheques from one bank to another.

In part, it was the Thatcher years which swept the gentlemanly old world of the City away. The 1980s saw the removal of old conventions which had served as barriers to competition. City folk still talk of the 'Big Bang' in 1986 – the stock market's abolition of rules about who does what and at what price in the market – as having revolutionized the way business was transacted. This change might seem at first glance to be rather a technical and undramatic innovation, but it led to a wave of mergers and acquisitions – brokers combining with brokers, banks buying brokers – and to a new era of much more aggressive trading practices.

But behind these particular reforms lies a still more fundamental reason for the death of the old City and for its rebirth in a modern guise. The real reason is the globalization of financial markets. Globalization occurred gradually over a period of twenty years. Until well into the 1970s financial markets, even in the world's largest centres, were oriented towards their own domestic economies. Money stayed at home. London was more outward looking than most, more so even than New York – and as for Frankfurt and Tokyo, although they were the financial centres of the world's most successful economies, their markets were modest affairs, of very little influence outside their own countries. But even London traders tended to regard their own markets – the London stock market and the British government bond market – as the centre of the universe. Each market, both in London and in other centres such as New York, had its own distinctive practices, conventions and rules. It was all very compartmentalized, and by present standards parochial.

In today's environment, however, money no longer faces any significant frontiers. It can move freely in search of the best return, from country to country, from continent to continent, and – what is more – it can do so instantaneously, at the speed of an electronic impulse. 'No man is an island' said John Donne four centuries ago. He meant it spiritually, of course. Yet today it has become true not just spiritually but in a very material sense, perhaps above all in the financial markets. What happens at one end of the world reverberates at the other immediately. Events in Tokyo affect London. News from New York affects London. In particular, the foreign exchange market is really just a single market, whether it is in Tokyo, London or New York; where the business is done depends on the time of day. The markets are increasingly like an ocean, stirred at different points by swirling currents and winds, but all one ocean none the less. There are no shallows or reaches uninfluenced by movements elsewhere.

One of the most important reasons for this globalization of the markets is that government rules and regulations have changed – and changed in a way which is now almost certainly irreversible. Over the last twenty years there has been a virtually uninterrupted trend of liberalization and deregulation of financial markets in all the major economies. Capital controls designed originally to prevent funds from leaving the domestic economy have been weakened or removed completely. Meanwhile, regulations restricting foreign competitors from competing in the domestic financial market – and thus allowing local institutions to have an easier time – have been simplified or dropped altogether.

The effect of these changes has been dramatic. The major financial centres have become crossroads where traders and financiers from all over the world meet to do business. In the City of London there are almost twice as many banks now as in 1970. There has been similar expansion in other financial centres such as Frankfurt and Tokyo. In this brutally competitive and international environment the City of London could no more carry on like a cosy club in the old way than the dinosaurs could afford to ignore climate changes and competition from the mammals. It had to open up – or risk extinction.

The other major new factor in the globalization of the markets (part cause and part effect of all this liberalization) has been the emergence of vast amounts of internationally footloose capital. Surplus funds from the economies of Europe, North America, Japan and – recently – other Asian countries now move from market to market, from country to country with fewer and fewer inhibitions: looking for short or long-term investment opportunities, switching between currencies on a phone call, put on deposit for a week or invested in thirty-year bonds at the snap of a finger. All of this is dramatically facilitated by information technology and telecommunications: powerful computers and complex data distribution systems which ensure that news and market information is available wherever there is a satellite dish and a power supply. Billions of dollars can be, and are, managed and invested from Caribbean islands or country cottages.

These funds are owned by a whole variety of players. They represent the reserves of governments, the savings and pension plans of individuals, cash balances and profits of banks and companies – all looking for a profitable home. If capital in earlier times was likely to stay at home, much more capital nowadays – even the private savings of individuals, and certainly the funds controlled by banks, insurance companies and pension funds – is ready to scour the world looking for investment opportunities which offer the best return.

In one sense, there is nothing new about all this. Throughout history humans have bartered and traded with each other. Money has been around for thousands of years and, as far as we know, humans have lent money to each other for most of that time. Banks have been around for hundreds of years (the oldest one still active today was founded in 1472 at Siena in Italy[1]). For much of that time, rich financiers have lent money to governments and financed trade across the oceans. Stocks in companies were being bought and sold in primitive stock markets in the eighteenth century, and financial markets of all kinds expanded rapidly in the nineteenth.

What is new about the last two decades is the sheer scale of the markets and the speed with which they are evolving. The flow of international capital has grown from a trickle to a flood which no government on earth could now dam. Gross capital outflows from the industrialized countries were about $850 billion in 1993, having averaged around $100 billion a year in the early 1980s – and much smaller amounts before that.

There are two basic outlets for the bulk of these funds: investment in stock (through which the investor buys a share in the ownership of companies) and in debt (in other words, where the investor lends to a borrower in return for interest).[2] Both these two alternatives are available in a whole variety of currencies, so that the investor faces a third basic choice – which currency to commit to. Hence, there are three basic financial markets – the stock markets, the bond (i.e. debt) markets and the foreign exchange market.

The goings-on in these three great markets of the City of London may seem very remote to individual men or women, who are more concerned about their job, mortgage, pension rights and cost of living than about the strange antics of City dealers. Yet the fact is that almost everyone will become involved – directly or indirectly – in these three markets at some time. Nowadays over 20 per cent of the adult population in Britain own shares (up from 3 per cent in 1979): the behaviour of the stock market affects them directly. Two-thirds of owner-occupiers have mortgages, and many more people have other forms of bank loan: every time money market rates of interest rise or fall, these changes feed through to the interest rate they have to pay. And each time we go on holiday abroad we change money and/or buy travellers' cheques, so that, in however small a way, we are affected directly by the currency markets. The markets also affect pensioners who are dependent on the interest rate on their savings or on share dividends; they affect consumers every time they buy something on credit or buy something imported. Share price movements, interest rate changes and currency swings all have a direct and pervasive affect on our lives. The financial markets, when they feature in the news, may seem distant and mysterious, but they affect us all.

They affect not only individuals, but companies

too, of course. Companies of all shapes and sizes use the markets and/or are exposed to their vagaries. Companies have much more complex demands for financial services than do individuals, however. Large companies in particular have many more choices. They can raise finance through the stock markets or through the debt markets. In raising debt, they may borrow short term on an overdraft, or they may borrow for much longer periods – at fixed or variable rates of interest – through the bond markets. And if they are exporters or importers they will be active in the foreign exchange markets, buying and selling currencies not only for immediate delivery but also for future delivery – in the 'forward market' – to cover future cash flows that arise in the course of their business.

So companies are exposed to the markets, just as individuals are. If they have overdrafts to finance their business, and interest rates rise, the result can be a profit collapse or even bankruptcy. Laker Airways – the popular 'people's' airline of the 1970s (it was the first to offer cut-price, no-frills scheduled flights to North America) – went spectacularly bankrupt in 1981 after borrowing in dollars whilst its income was largely in pounds. It was caught in a trap when the value of the dollar rose so sharply that the interest payments consumed more and more of its operating income. But even without that kind of currency mismatch, the market can set dangerous traps for companies. Between 1987 and 1988 interest rates in Britain rose from a low of 7.5 per cent to a high of 15 per cent. Over the following years, the number of bankruptcies rose from 10,500 in 1989 to over 24,000 in 1992 as the cost of borrowing doubled and recession squeezed demand for virtually all types of goods and services. All in all, companies know both the value and the dangers of the markets.

There are other users of the markets too. Apart from individuals and companies, there is one other major group of entities which is heavily dependent on the markets as a source of finance – governments. Throughout recorded history, governments have typically spent more than they can raise through taxation. They have resorted to various means of plugging the gap (often simply printing more money), but one of the most widespread means has been to borrow. They have borrowed from bankers – a practice which has often been disastrous for the banks (most recently in the 1970s, when huge amounts were lost by banks which lent to Latin-American countries[3]). They have also borrowed from their own citizens by issuing bonds in their own currencies. (Nowadays, British government bonds are bought by investors from all over the world, but that is a relatively recent phenomenon.) And in recent decades they have borrowed from the international markets through the issue of foreign currency bonds targeted at foreign investors.

The amounts involved are immense, and have tended to grow rapidly in the last three decades. Some countries – including some of the most wealthy – have seen the mountain of outstanding government debt grow larger than the annual output of their economies: Canada, Italy and Belgium have all found themselves in this position. Britain's government debt has grown less dramatically and has sometimes shrunk, but even so it remains very large (total debt outstanding in 1994 was £290 billion – just over half the size of Britain's annual output).

The use of the markets overall has thus grown enormously. Individual investors are there, looking for homes for capital; governments and companies are there, looking for finance. Both investors and borrowers use the foreign exchange market to slip effortlessly from one currency to another. And the banks are there – often as investors, occasionally to raise capital themselves (just like any other company) – but in addition, and crucially, in the distinctive role of *market-maker*.

Market-making is central to the functioning of modern financial markets. Markets need to function with enough orderliness and focus to ensure that buyers and sellers are enabled consistently to find the best match. In the housing market that role is performed by estate agents. In an auction, it is performed by the auctioneer. Only the most basic forms of market – a car-boot sale, for example – can do without it. In the case of the financial markets, the role is now virtually always performed by market-makers – banks which take upon themselves the responsibility of making prices on a two-way basis (i.e. quoting both sale and purchase prices), continuously and on demand from any counter-party who is in a position to transact. The market-makers do not, of course, do this out of altruism (any more than an estate agent does). Their purchase price (the 'bid') is always lower than their sale price (the 'offer'), thus allowing a profit margin on their turnover – although the margin is only as wide as the competition will permit. (In the foreign exchange market it is wafer-thin – less than 0.05 per cent.)

The way in which the life of a market-maker has evolved, from a gently paced administrative activity to the frenetic business of today, can be seen very clearly through developments in the foreign exchange market. From the end of the Second World War until 1972 the world's major currencies were controlled by an international system of fixed exchange rates. There were occasional devaluations, but these were rare, one-off changes intended to fix major economic problems, and always accompanied by big political crises. In between such upheavals, the price of the pound against the dollar, for example, did not change for years on end. Since 1972, when the system of rigid exchange rates was generally abandoned (having come under increasing strain as economic performance and conditions in the key countries diverged), the currencies have 'floated' – with varying degrees of government manipulation. The result has been a transformation of the market-making function into a highly risky business. Currency values now change from one day to the next – indeed, from minute to minute. The volume of trading has soared as participants seek to adjust their holdings constantly to exploit opportunities for gain and to avoid the risk of loss. The amounts involved have become astronomic. On an average day in London alone the amount of foreign exchange traded is equal to about half the annual gross national product of Britain. And the volume has doubled since 1989. The annual turnover in the foreign exchange market is over fifteen times the entire world's gross economic product.

The strain placed by all this on the dealers who work in bank dealing rooms can be immense. At times of particular turmoil, the demand to quote prices and transact deals can be unremitting; a dealer might be required to do over 200 deals per day, totalling well over £1 billion. But dealers are measured by the profits they earn, and the effect of price movement on a dealer's profit-and-loss position can be very uncomfortable indeed. Imagine what it must feel like to be a dealer who quoted a price in sterling to a large corporation, which has resulted in the company selling the bank £10 million, only to find the value of the pound is declining sharply because bad economic news has just come on the computer trading screen. No wonder this is regarded as one of the most stressful jobs there is.

Volatility is now a constant feature of life in the markets. Price movements of 2, 3 or even 4 per cent per day are not uncommon, whereas they would have been extremely rare in the 1970s. The opportunities for profit (and for loss) which are presented by such market behaviour are very large. The dealer in the example above stands to make – or lose – £100,000 for every 1 per cent move in the value of the pound. Such a move is easily possible within a single day – or even in five minutes. This is a market in which banks and companies which run 'open' positions (i.e. they are prepared to take a view that prices are going to move in a particular direction and to buy or sell accordingly) can make big profits – or run the risk of big losses.[4]

It is also a market in which the potential risk of loss through fraud or concealment by dealers is a trap for the unwary employer. The temptations created by the potential for gain or loss are legion. There is the temptation to run larger and larger positions when things are going right, or to 'double up' when things are going wrong (e.g. to buy more pounds when their price has already gone down, in the hope that the decline will be reversed and existing losses be more than offset by the resulting profits). Above all, there is the temptation to conceal the true position so as to hide losses from supervisors in the hope that they can be reversed through further trading before they are discovered. There are several examples of spectacular losses incurred by both banks and companies as a result of dealers digging themselves into a hole which gets deeper and deeper until it can no longer be concealed.[5]

There is, however, nothing new about financial market crises and scandals. They have occurred in all sorts of ways down the centuries, some of them quite bizarre. In the sixteenth century Holland was overtaken by an extraordinary frenzy of investment in tulip bulbs, which drove their price ever higher as people sank their life savings into these early growth stocks. And in the early eighteenth century Britain's gentry was rocked by the South Sea Bubble, a stock investment scam in which shares in a company founded to trade with the Spanish colonies in South America were sold on the basis of ludicrously rosy forecasts of profit potential. As ever, in both cases, those who got out before the music stopped made fortunes; those who didn't were ruined.[6] Barings, the blue-blooded merchant bank which collapsed in the wake of a futures trading scandal in 1995, had to be bailed out once before – in 1890, in the wake of huge losses on lending and investments in Latin America. Not much is new under the sun.

Moreover, the risks have grown more complex in recent years because trading techniques have become more complicated. We have seen the emergence of new kinds of trading – often involving highly sophisticated mathematical models. To take one example, the pound has a price in terms of dollars which can be fixed now for delivery at a future date (in the forward market). This forward price is simple to calculate, and forward currency markets have been in existence for many years. The new dimension is the ability to fix a price for the *option* (but not the obligation) to take delivery in the future. This may seem like a small and harmless modification, but in fact it brings into play some very complex mathematical modelling. Such products meet a real need: for instance, on the part of a contractor which has tendered for an overseas order and wants the option to cover the foreign currency cash flows if it should win the order, but not to have to exchange currencies if it fails to win it.

Options products of this kind often require dealers with strong mathematical abilities. Indeed, it is not uncommon to find mathematics or physics Ph.D.s sitting in dealing rooms, recruited solely to develop and trade such products. (They could not have done this before the advent in the 1980s of powerful personal computers.) Like any trading technique in the financial markets, the resulting products are a two-edged sword: they enable companies to cover themselves ever more precisely against market uncertainties which might otherwise undermine their business, or they provide further opportunities to take positions in the hope of making a profit from expected price movements. But their complexity makes them much more difficult to control and supervise. Thus the risks continue to multiply.

So the markets are still evolving; indeed, they will probably never reach a steady state. They will go on expanding in size and continue to grow in complexity. Computer power will continue to expand at a geometric rate, as it has done from the start, making ever faster and more complex calculations possible. Communications technology will also progress rapidly, bringing ever more information to the dealer. We are seeing the emergence of a veritable global bazaar – an on-line, real-time global market which allows a price to be put on almost anything, which is feverish and unceasing in its activity, and which is intrinsically volatile. The potential uses of the market are clear; so are its dangers. Whilst some might yearn to turn the clock back to the simpler, more predictable times in the 1950s and 1960s – before the days of high-profile City dealers, computers and complex mathematics – there is little reason to believe that anyone can now entice the genie back into the bottle.

All of this poses two fundamental questions for Christians: First, does all this activity contribute anything real to human welfare? At times, it looks like nothing more than a speculative whirlpool in which some get rich and others get poor. It seems as if the markets are constantly focused on the next five minutes only. What has this got to do with building human societies for the long term on a solid basis? And in any case, isn't the activity itself little more than a gambling casino? How could it possibly be the case that this bazaar has anything to do with the kingdom of God?

Secondly, what does it all do to the spiritual condition of those who work in the midst of it? How can it be right to devote such energy, talent and inventiveness to what amounts to nothing more than speculation? Making money out of speculating on price movements is making money out of nothing: how can this be right? What effect does it all have on the values of traders? If the most successful are those who are obsessive in their commitment to and fascination with trading, does the system not, in effect, give whisky to an alcoholic? Despite all their bonuses and flash lifestyles, do they pay too high a price? We shall explore these issues in the following chapters.

NOTES

1 The evocatively named Banco dei Monte da Paschi di Siena – the bank of the hillside pastures of Siena – is the oldest bank.

2 There is a third outlet: investment in the commodity markets – precious metals such as gold or silver, and natural resources such as oil and copper. However, these markets are relatively less important as outlets for international capital funds seeking investment.

3 In so doing, they relied too much on the principle – enunciated in a notorious maxim of a former Chairman of Citicorp, the great New York bank – that countries, unlike corporations, could not go bankrupt since they always had the power of taxation to raise the necessary funds to meet repayment schedules. What the banks found out, however, was that countries could indeed go bankrupt – not in a legal sense, but by simply defaulting – and that when they did so the banks concerned had very little means of redress. The result was that a number of major banks themselves very nearly went bankrupt.

4 It is often believed that such position-taking must be a zero-sum game: if one institution makes a profit, others must have made an equal loss. By implication, moreover, this is an activity which is assumed to be of no net value to the economy. In fact, however, although there are plenty of occasions when those who take such positions make losses, it is not necessarily the case that all the pluses

and minuses add up to zero. And the potential value to the economy of such position-taking is in forcing prices to adjust more quickly to correct real imbalances of supply and demand. Market speculation by no means always has a beneficial effect, but it certainly can do so. See Chapter 4 for the example of what many consider to have been the real benefit to the British economy of the large-scale market pressure which built up against the British pound in 1992.

5   The last ten years have seen major losses incurred through trading, running into the hundreds of millions, by a London merchant bank, by a New York investment house and by large multinational companies. This is not a business for the faint-hearted; and the market punishes those who do not supervise their traders effectively.

6   As the South Sea Bubble began finally to collapse – which, like all such schemes, it did with frightening speed – Members of Parliament were loud in their condemnation of the way in which it had 'diverted the genius of the nation from trade and industry' into worthless financial speculation. It is a charge which has been levelled at the City of London many times since.

2

The Root of All Evil?

The financial markets have had a bad press with the public at large from time immemorial. This isn't surprising, since the ordinary citizen's contact with finance was exclusively through the small-time money-lender or pawnbroker. Not until well into the twentieth century was credit a means of buying a consumer luxury such as a new car or a summer holiday. In earlier times, credit was a lifeline when drowning in hard times – and a lifeline which was notoriously expensive. People borrowed when the harvest failed or when the bread-winner went sick: they borrowed only when they were desperate. And they went to a money-lender who knew they were in his power because they were in grave difficulty. Those who failed to repay found themselves in prison, from which there was often no way out. Dickens's novel *Little Dorrit* is a graphic description of the dilemma of those who became trapped by debt.

This bitter experience of the power of money is reflected in the attitude of the Christian Church to the financial markets down the centuries. From very early times, Christian teaching has treated money as the root of all sorts of social evil. Church teaching until at least the fifteenth century held that usury – taking interest on loans – was quite simply contrary to the law of God. For a thousand years of Christian history, in fact, not a single voice of any significance was raised against this view. Augustine – writing in the early fifth century, and probably the only early Christian thinker who is known at all widely to a modern Christian audience – bluntly called usury a crime. Thomas Aquinas, the brilliant and widely influential systematizer of medieval thought, shared the view that taking interest in any form was morally wrong. The Protestant Luther also shared this view – in fact, if anything, he held it even more forcefully. For him, usury was so wrong that money-lenders deserved to be excommunicated and should be denied a Christian burial. 'The greatest misfortune of the nation is easily the traffic in interest ... the devil invented it.'[1]

Yet the Church leaders did not get their hostility directly from anything Jesus said or did. Jesus had plenty to say about wealth and its effects on its owners. He knew how wealth could become an obsession which cramped the spiritual life. He knew that people could give too much to the task of accumulation of riches, and in so doing put at risk their souls. It was easier for a camel to go through the eye of a needle than for the rich to enter the kingdom of heaven. But Jesus had little to say about commerce as such. He cast out the money-changers from the temple, undoubtedly; but this was clearly a protest against corruption in the religious establishment, not against finance and money as such. Jesus in fact mentions banks and interest only once – in the parable of the talents, when the reference to interest is entirely neutral and without any suggestion of disapproval (see Matthew 25:27).

Nor did the hostility come directly or indirectly from Paul. He calls for total commitment to Christ and for sacrificial generosity to fellow Christians, but there is no sign that he expected Christians not to follow normal trades. And he is silent about the merits of commerce and finance *per se*. In the first letter to Timothy, it is the love of money – not money as such – which is the root of all kinds of evil (see 1 Timothy 6:10).

It was the Old Testament which provided rather clearer instruction on trading and money. The problem of indebtedness was, of course, much older than Christianity, and Christian teaching accordingly drew deep from wells older than itself. Money-lending had been a means of exploiting those in distress for many centuries before Christ was born. The kind of stories Dickens told about nineteenth-century England had parallels, in a simpler and more agricultural setting, thousands of years before in Israel. The smallholder who became a debtor because the harvest failed started down a slippery slope. The debtor became a tenant; and tenancy drifted into slavery. It was a path trodden by countless families. The ability to provide finance was inexorably associated with increasing wealth; the need to borrow led to poverty and slavery.

Israel's law – which by any standards was an extraordinary phenomenon – explicitly tackled the problems of debt and poverty in a variety of ways. It was astonishingly – perhaps, in fact, uniquely for its time – concerned to protect the weaker members of the community. And it was ambitiously imaginative in how it proposed to deal with the problem. A whole range of measures to prevent the accumulation of too much wealth in too few hands, and to take the edge off economic hardship, is announced in the law books of the Old Testament.

The core of this law, so far as credit and capital were concerned, was that land – the only fixed capital of the time – could not be bought and sold in perpetuity, but only for a maximum of forty-nine years. Its price was fixed in relation to the number of harvests that would be obtained – in other words, land should be sold on a leasehold basis, with the price reflecting the number of years' profit remaining in the lease. This principle was buttressed by other measures to prevent undue exploitation of the distressed by the powerful. Any creditor holding security over someone else's goods must release the debtor from his pledge on the seventh year – in other words, financial obligations should not last for ever. A lender should not take someone's mill or millstone as security, for that would be to remove an essential of life itself (their ability to make bread). In other words, no one should be mortgaged so heavily that their very livelihood is put at risk. In addition, wages must be paid when due: since the labourer is poorer than the employer, he should not be forced, in effect, to give the employer credit. And no one should move their boundary markers – i.e. expand their land-holdings at the expense of others; nor should they use false weights for measuring produce purchased or sold; and so on.

Every one of these provisions is a clue to a practice that must have been widespread in the society of the time.

Credit was clearly a means of amassing power and reducing fellow citizens to dependency or even to outright slavery. The theory was that all Israelites were the people of God, and were equal and free. But debt, impoverishment and slavery were in fact so common that the law did the next best thing: it sought to regulate the situation in order to limit the hardship. The ideal was that lending between citizens of Israel should be free of interest (see Deuteronomy 23:20). But in practice, the law limited its objective to prohibiting loans *to the distressed* from carrying interest: 'If your brother becomes impoverished and cannot support himself in the community, you will assist him as you would a stranger or a guest ... Do not charge him interest on a loan, but fear your God and let your brother live with you' (Leviticus 25:35–36). (Here, as elsewhere in the law books of the Old Testament, the term 'brother' has a wide connotation: it meant not only a literal brother, but by extension anyone who was of the people of God.)

Again, the ideal was that no citizen of Israel should be reduced to slavery. In practice, however, it was so common that even the Ten Commandments include provisions for ensuring reasonable treatment of slaves.[2] In particular, the law provided that slavery should never be permanent: 'If your brother becomes impoverished ... and sells himself to you, you will not make him do the work of a slave; you will treat him like an employee or guest, and he will work for you until the jubilee year' (Leviticus 25:39–40) – i.e. until that same forty-ninth year when land reverted to its original owner, at which time your brother would be free to leave you and regain possession of his own ancestral land.

Despite the perceptiveness and pragmatism of the law, there is no evidence that its key principles were ever implemented. In particular, there is no sign that the jubilee year system was ever put into effect. It is never mentioned in any of the history books of the Old Testament, and all the indications are that over time, land-holdings became more and more concentrated. Whatever the pattern may have been when Israel was evolving from a nomadic into an agricultural society in the very early days, it is clear that by the time of the settled Israelite state under David and Solomon and later (from about a thousand years before Christ), the country had become like medieval Europe. Powerful families controlled vast land-holdings and dominated the lives of large numbers of people – retainers, tenants and slaves.

This state of affairs brought forth savage criticism in the form of the outcry by the prophets. These strange, lonely, uncomfortable figures are the crowning glory of Israelite history. They emerged from all sorts of backgrounds to draw attention – often in words of the most plaintive and haunting beauty – to the huge gulf which existed between the pretensions evidenced in the law and the actual circumstances of life. So far as capital accumulation and the oppression of the poor were concerned, the most bitter attack came from Amos, a figure who emerged in about 760 BC. Amos did not come from an aristocratic or powerful background; he seems to have been an ordinary farmer. His message was simple, straightforward and bleak: social oppression and religious hypocrisy were so bad that disaster was coming.

Therefore, because you trample on the poor
and take from them levies of grain;
you have built houses of hewn stone,
but you shall not live in them;
you have planted pleasant vineyards,
but you shall not drink their wine.
(Amos 5:11)

Hear this, you that trample on the needy,
and bring to ruin the poor of the land,
saying, ' When will the new moon be over
so that we may sell grain;
and the Sabbath,
so that we may offer wheat for sale?
We will make the ephah small and the shekel
great,
and practice deceit with false balances,
buying the poor for silver
and the needy for a pair of sandals,
and selling the sweepings of the wheat.'
... ' On that day' says the Lord God,
' I will make the sun go down at noon,
and darken the earth in broad daylight.
I will turn your feasts into mourning,
and all your songs into lamentation;
I will bring sackcloth on all loins,
and baldness on every head;
I will make it like the mourning for an only son,
and the end of it like a bitter day.'
(Amos 8:4–6, 9–10)

Notice in particular how the attack on the economically powerful widens out to include not only the accumulation of land and the gaudy palaces, but also their exploitative and fraudulent trading practices. The angry dissidents of nineteenth- and twentieth-century Europe could not have said it better.

The voices of the prophets went largely unheeded, but not unrecorded. The interplay of law and prophets with the progress of Israelite history, as reflected in the pages of the Old Testament, provided all the ammunition the Christian theologians needed later on as they wrestled with exactly the same social trends. So far as they were concerned, the law was clear: lending at interest was wrong; so was any form of trade that profited from another's misfortune. As Luther put it, 'A person should not say "I will sell as dear as I can" but rather "I will sell as is right and proper". You should not sell according to your own will, as if you were a god. Because selling is something you do to your neighbour, it should be restrained within the limits of law and conscience, so that you may do so without injury to your neighbour.' [3]

The suspicion of commerce and finance was further underpinned by the philosophical outlook Christian thought derived from classical Greek thinkers – notably Aristotle, whose influence on medieval thought was profound. For Aristotle, writing 350 years before Christ, the only natural – and therefore morally acceptable – form of commerce was barter. Exchange of goods is natural because it enables the parties to the exchange to satisfy their natural requirements. But as soon as money is introduced into the process, it tends to become an end in itself

– which is unnatural, because money itself gives no satisfaction. Wealth can only be a means to an end; there is nothing either natural or worthy about the creation of financial wealth. Aristotle considered even retail trade to be unnatural because it involved profit at another's expense. But in his view usury was the worst form of commerce because it involved profit from money itself – from the medium of exchange rather than from real goods.

Buried in this set of attitudes is a belief that there is a fair or 'just' price for any product, based on the cost of raw materials and the cost of labour. This belief was based on the assumption that it was possible to determine *a priori* what labour ought to earn, depending on its status in society. That in turn was enough to determine the price at which trade should take place, since everything was made from labour and raw materials (and the price of the raw materials was in turn determined by the labour involved in their production). If goods were sold at a higher price, this was unnatural profit. There was no understanding that capital might have to be invested and that capital might have a cost. So lending money to make money was rejected as doubly unnatural (profit itself was bad enough, but profit from money was beyond the pale). And to hold anything to be unnatural was the ultimate Aristotelian condemnation.

Thus the Christian attitude to commerce and finance was formed on the basis of a Jewish heritage which considered it exploitative, and buttressed by a Greek world-view, according to which it was unnatural. No wonder the result was so unmistakably hostile. Christian thought envisaged – as did older Jewish and Greek theory – a simple world in which credit ought to play no real part.

If a neighbouring family fell on hard times, you supported them; you did not lend at interest. If you sold produce you did so at the just price, which covered your costs and represented a reasonable return on the labour involved. The price of labour itself was assumed fixed – theoretically equal, but in practice dependent on your station in society. Though some were more equal than others, there should be no exploitation of misfortune.

One ironic – and sinister – by-product of all this was to put the Jews of Europe in the position of being the main money-lenders and bankers of the Christian world. Both the Jews and the Christians accepted, in theory at least, the prohibition on lending at interest *to their own brothers* (meaning others of the same faith). That meant that a good Christian did not lend to a Christian, but might borrow from a Jew. Since the Jews were largely banned from all normal crafts and activities, and since there was a perennial demand for credit by all strata of Christian society, the result was that finance came to be a profession in which Jews were prominent. Given the intrinsic unpopularity of finance, and the hostile teaching of the Church on usury, the effect was to give dangerous impetus to anti-Semitism throughout Europe. The figure of Shylock in Shakespeare's play *The Merchant of Venice* is powerful testimony to the fear and loathing heaped on Jews – as much as anything because of their role in the forbidden but lucrative sphere of finance. As Shylock says, when the merchant Antonio comes to him for a loan:

> *Signor Antonio, many a time and oft,*
> *In the Rialto, you have rated me*

> *About my moneys, and my usances:*
> *Still have I borne it with a patient shrug;*
> *For sufferance is the badge of all our tribe.*
> *You call me misbeliever, cut-throat dog,*
> *And spit upon my Jewish gaberdine,*
> *And all for use of that which is mine own.*
> *Well then, it now appears, you need my*
> *help ...* (I. iii. 105–13)

The story of *The Merchant of Venice* is preposterous enough, but it catches the essence of a relationship of hostile convenience which sowed seeds that bore frightful fruit in the twentieth century.

Christian attitudes to commerce and finance could not continue in this mould as trade began to flourish, especially from the fifteenth century onwards. Initially, somewhat reluctantly, distinctions began to be drawn between lending at interest – still regarded as unacceptable – and investment, where the risk was shared by the investor as well as the entrepreneur. It was Calvin – the cold and lucid theologian (and *de facto* ruler) of Protestant Geneva – who made the real break with the past. Unlike Luther, who always remained conservative and rural in his sympathies and instincts, Calvin was an urban figure, more in tune with the aspirations of the new urban trading classes.

Calvin dealt with the old orthodoxy about the morality of finance quite simply. He stated bluntly that the Old Testament law had applied to the ancient society of the Israelites but was no longer relevant because a new Christian dispensation was now in effect. The new law was a law of love. By this test plenty of lending was indeed wrong, because it exploited the poor. But there could be no objection to loans at reasonable rates between parties who had good business reasons to lend and to borrow respectively:

> *Usury is not now unlawful, except insofar as*
> *it contravenes equity and brotherly union.*
> *Let each one, then, place himself before*
> *God's judgement seat, and not do to his*
> *neighbour what he would not have done to*
> *himself, from which a sure and infallible*
> *decision may be come to.*[4]

This shift was a radical one – although, of course, it stopped a long way short of a gospel for a free market. It was accompanied by an equally radical shift in the concept of vocation. In the medieval world, the concept of vocation had effectively been reserved to clerical careers. Luther made room for the idea that there were Christian 'callings' to secular roles as well, but he was still enough a part of the medieval world to limit his understanding of what constituted a 'calling' to roles that were part of a largely agricultural and craft-based economy. Farmers and craftsmen might be following a vocation, but not financiers and entrepreneurs. Calvin, on the other hand, broke out of this simple mould by resorting to the notion of stewardship. If you had money, this was a gift from God, of which you were a steward and which was given to be used. This was a fundamental shift and meant that investment and banking could be spiritually legitimate activities. Finance could be considered a calling; money-lenders could come in from the cold.

However, this did not mean that they could do what they liked. There was an obligation of hard work and integrity. And the Geneva government set clear limits to economic licence: traders were regularly censured for extortion, monopolistic practices and fraud. Calvin in fact sought a balance. He shifted Christian teaching on economics and finance in the direction required to make sure that it could be meaningfully applied to an urban and commercial society, without remaining stuck in a medieval system, but he sought to retain the guiding principle of the law of love: we should not prey on the weak or exploit those in distress. Wealth is a gift, not a right; and service is the dominant motivating theme.

Yet the risk was that this would prove to be a half-way house. Calvin's was an attempt in effect to focus on the spirit, rather than the letter, of the law. He was not hobbled by the old Aristotelian view of what was either 'natural' or 'unnatural', and he did not consider the modern Christian world bound by the details of the old Jewish law. But he certainly considered Christians to be under the law as ratified by Christ. Christ's summary of the law (or rather, statement of the essence of the law) had two basic requirements – to love the Lord God with all one's power, and to love one's neighbour as oneself. From these requirements came the obligation of stewardship of God's gifts and of service to others. For Calvin, both these ideals were to inform every aspect of commercial and financial activity.

This view of commerce did not allow any central role for competition. Calvin was still enough of a child of the medieval world to think in terms of a just price for goods and for labour. Hence, commercial excellence was derived not from competitive advantage, but from striving to serve by using the resources the Lord gives to the maximum. In Calvin's scheme of things, commercial and financial success was wholly consistent with serving the community.

It was not long before two more crucial mental leaps followed, which seemed to cut commerce and finance completely free from the constraints applied by Christian theology. The first was made by philosophers of the early seventeenth century, who began to argue a point that seems obvious nowadays but which was then revolutionary. There is no such thing as a 'just price' for anything, it was said. Goods (and labour) are worth whatever price is agreed for them by a buyer and a seller negotiating freely in the market. This brought the focus of theory onto the market. No longer was the market just a meeting-point where people bought and sold at a predeterminable just price. The market was suddenly the mechanism for price-making. If Calvin's shift was a big one, this was a bigger one still.

The next leap was that of the great Scottish economist Adam Smith, who brought to centre stage at last the phenomenon of *competition*. Its existence had of course been recognized from the first, but it had been condemned as nothing but combative greed – a motive totally inconsistent with the spirit of Christian life. No one had thought of anything so perverse as to elevate competition to the status of usefulness, let alone that of worthiness. Adam Smith, whilst avoiding the question of its intrinsic worthiness, quite openly put the role of competition in the market-place at the centre of commercial transactions and of economic progress.

The implications of the shift from the medieval consensus through Calvin to Smith were profound. On the face of it, the shift left Christianity with nothing to say about the world of commerce and finance. According to Adam Smith, the markets operated by their own internal laws which pulled off the conjuring act of using an unworthy motive (competitive greed) to allocate goods and services with maximum efficiency:

> It is not from the benevolence of the
> butcher, the brewer or the baker that we
> expect our dinner; but from their regard to
> their own interest. We address ourselves
> not to their humanity but to their self-love.[5]

This is poles apart from Calvin's understanding of the motive force of commerce and finance. With Adam Smith, the market moved from pariah to panacea. There need be no more nonsense about usury being unnatural, or about there being just prices for all goods and services; no more need to regulate market prices to prevent extortion. In fact, the tables were turned. Cocking a snook (perhaps unconsciously) at Aristotle, Edmund Burke – the great British parliamentarian of the late eighteenth century – commented that 'The laws of commerce are the laws of nature, and therefore the laws of God.' What had been pronounced unnatural by Aristotle was on the contrary natural, and therefore consistent with the divine order.

The change was complete by the end of the

eighteenth century. The claim of Christian theology to restrain and regulate the markets seemed to have gone for good. It was not so much that the Church lost power and influence (it still retained considerable influence until well into the twentieth century – as was demonstrated, for example, in the debate about Sunday trading), but the real danger was that it had no answer to Adam Smith. Not on a theoretical plane, at least. If the market set prices solely on the basis of supply and demand, who was to say what was extortionate? How could the issue of commercial right and wrong even get onto the agenda? The Christian Church appeared to have lost its time-honoured framework of principles for commercial morality. The markets had usurped their place.

At the practical level, there was of course plenty to say about the ill-effects of the market as manifested in the Britain of the Industrial Revolution. Child labour, inhuman factory conditions, social squalor and private riches provided plenty of ammunition for latter-day prophets with the instincts and rhetoric of an Amos. But the only serious *theoretical* challenge to the philosophy of the amoral market was mounted not by the Christian Church, but by Karl Marx.

For Marx, the important actors in the drama were not individuals negotiating freely in the market-place – an idea which he regarded as tendentious fiction – but classes. The working class sold its labour power to the capitalists for too little, because the capitalists had the power which came from ownership whilst the workers were disunited. As a result, the surplus value created by labour power (i.e. profit) was creamed off by the capitalist owners. Since the capitalists had no God-given right to ownership of capital (at some point in the historical process it had been seized from the people by the capitalist class), the remedy was clear: rectifying this injustice required the expropriation of the expropriators.[6]

The intriguing historical 'might-have-been' is the question of what would have happened if the Christian Church had adopted some version of this theory. Marx was, of course, hostile to religion, but this hostility was in no way intrinsic to his theory. And Marxism has, after all, clear echoes of the medieval just price theory, and of the whole Jewish/Christian attitude to profit and usury. If there is a nineteenth-century voice who sounds most like Amos, it is quite certainly Karl Marx – except that where Amos looked to God to bring justice, Marx looked to the working class to seize their destiny for themselves. But the Church did not develop any authoritative new economic model or commercial morality. There were some prominent Christian socialists, but the Church as a whole was not behind them.

Marxism was instead taken over by Lenin – under whom it was used to create a powerful centralist machine, which was in turn used to devastating effect under Stalin. By the late 1980s the whole experiment was obviously collapsing. Its end was lamented by few – though many remain traumatized. Meanwhile, society in all countries – whether ex-communist or not – seems to lack any sense of common purpose. In the realm of commerce and finance, the market is the default option; in the absence of alternative norms and mechanisms, the market rules. Adam Smith has outlived Karl Marx after all.

Yet the Christian Church has for the most part been unable to come to terms with the financial markets, even though there were certainly many Christians in the eighteenth and nineteenth centuries who were deeply engaged in commerce and who regarded free trade as compatible with, and indeed supportive of, the advance of Christian civilization. The hostility is deep-rooted, both at the theoretical and practical levels. For one thing, the Church has never been able to accept the idea that the real worth of people or things might be determined solely by supply and demand. It seems intrinsically absurd – as well as scandalous – that, for example, a young City of London dealer should be able to earn ten or more times as much as the head of a large comprehensive school. Yet when the Church makes this point, it is often frustrated to find that the more fanatical devotees of the market simply respond by intoning the words 'supply and demand' like some kind of litany.

In its instinctive revulsion, the Church at least sometimes finds support in broad public attitudes. Even the notion of a just price for goods and services occasionally strikes a resonant chord. At an auction in London, for example, an auctioneer tried on one occasion to start the bidding for an exquisite Persian carpet of shimmering colour and beauty at £1,000. He could not get a bid and had to start much lower. As the bidding ran out of breath at £800 he was heard to plead '*Surely* it's worth more than that ... *Look* at all the intricate work!' Without knowing it, that auctioneer was echoing the medieval Church's theory that there is a just price for everything, based on the amount of labour involved. That theory would have held that the morning's sale price for the carpet was indeed below its real worth. Yet market theory disagrees. It holds that in such circumstances there is no other evidence of real worth than the price agreed between buyer and seller. That day, as the carpet went under the hammer, it was clear that the heart of the audience was with the auctioneer's lament but their heads (or cheque books) were with Adam Smith.

Christianity has never come to terms with competition either. There is a deep-seated feeling that competition is aggressive, materialistic and inconsistent with the law of love. It may be natural (as recognized by those eighteenth-century thinkers); it may even be consistent with a Darwinian view of progress being achieved through the survival of the fittest. But how can it be reconciled with the ethic of the New Testament?

> Beloved, let us love one another, because
> love is from God; everyone who loves is born
> of God and knows God. Whoever does not
> love does not know God, for God is love ...
> Beloved, since God loved us so much, we
> ought also to love one another. No one has
> ever seen God; if we love one another, God
> lives in us, and his love is perfected in us.
> (1 John 4:7–8, 11–12)

It is hard to see how this can be reconciled with competitiveness. How can Christians be called to a life of commerce in general – or finance in particular – since competition is part of the very essence of such a life? How can you be *called* to work in the markets? The dilemma is made all the more acute because so much of the activity of the markets looks like pure speculation, which in turn simply feels like a polite word for gambling. Archbishop William Temple, one of the most influential Anglican church leaders of the period after the First World War, expressed this very general concern as follows:

> When the necessary work of society is so organized as to make the acquisition of wealth the chief criterion of success, it encourages a feverish scramble for money, and false respect for the victors in the struggle, which is as fatal in its moral consequences as any other form of idolatry.[7]

So the Church has often felt more comfortable keeping the markets at bay. It has always felt that it could smell the scent of evil about them. If at all possible, it would prefer to find alternatives to them which would be more obviously compatible with Christian ideals. At the very least, it has wanted to see them subordinated to strict regulation, both to ensure that they serve the public good and to protect the disadvantaged.

Some Christian writers are not merely reserved about the markets, they see them as entirely antithetical to Christian standards and to human welfare. As a recent example of thoroughgoing hostility to the markets and all that they stand for, Timothy Gorringe, writing from the vantagepoint of an Oxford chaplaincy, envisages a 'realistic alternative' that will

> *involve – as Deuteronomy, the medieval theologians and Luther all insisted – the abolition of usury. The charging of interest, it has been shown, involves a significant transfer of wealth to the richest groups of a country's population. This systematic transfer of money from those who need it most to those who need it least is one of the factors pushing the world towards catastrophe. It fuels the urge of the very rich, including the huge industrial and financial corporations, to compete with one another purely for the sake of economic wealth and power. It lulls the moderately well off into a complacent sense that all is well with economic life. By artificially increasing the pressures on the less well off and the poor, it deepens their economic dependency. In each of these ways it stimulates an unnecessarily high level of economic activity and the ecological damage which results. Thus interest is opposed for the very reason it was opposed by the medieval Church – because it harms life.*[8]

Gorringe represents an extreme point of view amongst Christian writers on the markets, but many Christian clergy and theologians would have at least some sympathy with his yearning for a better way. The Christian Church knows what it does not like or trust, but the search for a better way has proved elusive and sometimes shows signs of a longing to return to a lost medieval thought-world.

Gorringe, for example, draws extensively on political and economic theory as well as on Jewish and Christian moral theology. But he takes little account of the realities of the commercial and financial world. His is a moving vision, perhaps, but it is of no help to wish that the world might become the sort of communitarian idyll that it never was, even in medieval times.

In the meantime, Christian writers often have little practical knowledge of what to say to those who work in the midst of it all. In general, the Church has been more ready to talk about the moral issues involved in the distribution of wealth than to grapple with the specific dilemmas involved in the creation of wealth – particularly when it comes to the question of the role of finance in the creation of wealth.

There are, however, some encouraging signs in recent years of an attempt by Christians to react more constructively to the world of finance. Gerald Priestland, a popular Christian journalist and broadcaster, wrote as follows about the City of London:

> Bring together the world of money and the world of big impersonal organizations and there are generated the poisoned images of capitalism, imperialism, neo-colonialism and the transnational corporations – all of which it is fashionable to boo. Yet none of these trends has been wholly evil; most of them, from a broad view, have produced a considerable balance of good ...[9]

On a rather more academic plane, John Atherton writes a carefully balanced appraisal of the pluses and minuses of a free market in his book *Faith in the Nation*, which was published during the apogee of the Thatcher revolution in 1988.[10] And the Archbishop of Canterbury, Dr George Carey – for whom the strengthening of the Church's ability to speak intelligently to the world of commerce has become an important goal – has specifically addressed the financial markets, calling for a realistic appreciation of their role:

> *If one cosy [Christian] myth is that business is somehow inherently smutty, another is that 'real work' is making things whereas the really questionable activity is 'financial wheeler-dealing'. This is absurd. It is impossible to conceive of an advanced real economy without a sophisticated financial sector. If our economy partly depends on an efficient market in capital, shares, foreign currency and the like, it is preposterous to talk of the sector as if it is basically anti-social, however we may wish to challenge particular aspects of its operations. It is contrary to Christian morality ... to withdraw human understanding from any group of our fellow citizens and prefer to nurture our own crude stereotypes instead.*[11]

So the pendulum has swung a considerable way in the last twenty years or so. But it is still true that for many Christian theologians, and for the vast majority of parish clergy and preachers, the markets remain either a theoretical construct or a 'black box'. As a result, the Church has little to say that is of practical relevance to those who actually work in them.

Yet there is a gospel to proclaim to those who work in the commercial and financial world. That gospel cannot be based on a fastidious dislike of the whole business of trading in money; it needs to be based on real experience if it is to ring true. This is not the same thing as saying that the Church has no right to be critical of the workings of the financial world, of course. Although it is pointless (not to say hypocritical, since everyone is involved in them to some degree) to condemn the markets roundly as immoral, the Church can never agree to treat them as purely amoral. But we have to remember that Christ's message is proclaimed from amongst people, not from a distance, and on the basis of shared experience.

The markets are a fact of life. Some look for a third way other than the market and Marxism, but there is no third way – at least not by the start of the next working week. The third way looks all too often like a wish to model our world on an idealized past, but we live in the world as it is now and we have to go to work in it. That means that we need to find the kingdom of God in the midst of the markets. To do this, Christians need to understand them and accept involvement. On the basis of that involvement, we need to give our answers to the questions posed at the end of the last chapter. Does the activity of the markets contribute to the kingdom of God? And what does it do to those who work there?

NOTES

1 'To the Christian Nobility', *Luther's Works* (Erlangen edition) VI, p. 466.

2 See Exodus 20:10, which provides for a Sabbath rest not only for the family, but for the household slaves – and indeed for the livestock.

3 *Luther's Works* (Erlangen edition) XV, p. 295.

4 See B. Nelson, *The Idea of Usury* (University of Chicago Press, 1969), pp. 75ff., as cited in Richard Harries, *Is There a Gospel for the Rich?* (London: Mowbray, 1992), p. 140.

5 Adam Smith, *The Wealth of Nations*, book I, ch. 2.

6 Marx also argued that the capitalist class would eventually self-destruct as a result of internecine competition. In his major work *Das Kapital*, he is content to forecast the end of capitalism as a historical inevitability. In other writings, notably in *The Communist Manifesto*, he calls for the workers of the world to unite and seize their birthright.

7 Michael Novak, *The Spirit of Democratic Capitalism* (London: IEA Health and Welfare Unit, 1991), p. 35.

8 Timothy Gorringe, *Capital and the Kingdom* (London: SPCK, 1994), p. 167.

9 Gerald Priestland, *Priestland Right and Wrong* (London: Collins, 1983), p. 59.

10 John Atherton, *Faith in the Nation: A Christian Vision for Britain* (London: SPCK, 1988), pp. 57–60.

11 Dr George Carey, in an address to the Manchester Business School, delivered in November 1994.

3

A Month in the City

Many people feel instinctively that the financial markets are little more than a casino – a casino, furthermore, in which some players have marked cards and are out to break the bank. Surely it would be better, so many might argue who are bewildered by the turmoil of the markets, if prices of such commodities as bonds, stocks and foreign exchange were set by public policy. Wise people with computerized modelling and research capabilities, acting in the public interest, could surely do a better job than a mêlée of rapacious traders. How, in fact, could we ever consider the financial markets as we know them in reality to be part of the kingdom of God?

To understand why there is no practical alternative to the markets, why there is no real possibility of avoiding them and relying instead on some form of administrative machinery operating in the public interest, we need to begin by looking at what actually goes on in them. We need to understand what it feels like when viewed from the midst of it all. For the markets are not like a game of roulette or poker, with fixed rules and known probabilities. The truth is that the interplay of forces which determines the value of currencies, bonds and stocks from one day to the next is infinitely complex. Relationships between variables are uncertain and impermanent. No mathematical modelling and forecasting, however intricate, can substitute effectively for the balancing of a million interests in the market-place. This balancing process is never-ending, interlinked and unpredictable. It never settles down to an equilibrium; one thing affects another, as a snooker ball sends a dozen others scurrying in different directions; and life is full of surprises, great and small.

The best way to see this is to look at the workings of the market at one particular moment in its never-ending history; to look at it as specific events unfold, without any knowledge of what happened afterwards. This chapter looks at what was going on in the month of May 1995. Not because that month was especially striking: on the contrary, none of the currents which moved the markets that month were of the dramatic kind which get headlines on the TV news. It was, in fact, a normal month, and provides for that reason a good example of the ebb and flow of influences on human commercial affairs. It was a normal month, that is, in the sense that it exhibited the usual mix of forces, and posed – and left unanswered – the usual questions about what would happen next. May 1995 was chosen simply because it happened to be the month in which I started writing this book.

Four main questions were the talk of the markets in May 1995. No one knew the answers – not the governments, not the banks involved, not the financial pundits of the *Financial Times* and *The Economist* (the City's two most influential oracles). But everyone had opinions. Some were to be proven wrong quickly – or was it just that their timing was wrong? They would have to wait and see. As Harold Wilson, the former Prime Minister, once said, a week is a long time in politics. He might have added that the same is true of the markets. And a month is an eternity.

1. Was the pound about to crash (again)?

Since its unceremonious ejection from the European Exchange Rate Mechanism (the ERM) in September 1992, the pound had slid sharply from its original ERM rate of 2.95 German marks to the pound. After a bumpy ride down, it had settled on a new plateau of around 2.50.

Since then the British economy had been doing well. The competitive exchange rate was a boost to exports, and interest rates were declining because it was no longer necessary to keep them high to support the old exchange rate. As a result, the economy was picking up and unemployment was falling. But consumer demand remained weak – surprisingly so on the face of it, until it was recognized how shaken the consumer had been by the loss of job security and the collapse of the housing market. So imports were not being sucked into the economy, and a period of robust growth without a balance-of-payments crisis or an explosion of inflation (the twin torments of the British economy for a whole generation) seemed to be under way. From an economist's point of view, this all looked extraordinarily healthy. By late 1994, the British had low interest rates, declining unemployment and the strongest growth rate of any of the major European economies.

But there was one catch. The very thing that made the economists so pleased – the weakness of consumer demand – was cause and effect of a lack of confidence and morale which brought the Conservative government down to unprecedented depths of unpopularity. With each passing by-election, the government's already thin majority was further diminished. Its future looked bleak – all the more so when its tired and grey image was contrasted with the bright new look of the rejuvenated Labour Party.

Then the pound started to slide again during the early weeks of 1995 – partly because the dollar was weakening against the mighty German mark (and the dollar always tends to drag the pound down with it[1]), but also because of niggling concerns about the weakness of the British government. The Bank of England had started to raise interest rates as a pre-emptive measure to avoid any chance of inflation rising as unemployment fell further. However, although raising interest rates might well be the correct recipe, it would do nothing at all for the government's popularity.

The markets began to sniff trouble. How much further would rates have to rise to keep inflation subdued? Hawks were determined that the right choice was to err on the side of caution: rates should go higher, since the sleeping demon should not be allowed to stir at any price. Doves took the view that the rises of the previous six months were already working their medicine and that growth was already slowing. But no one could be sure. How far would the renewed weakness of the pound compound the problem, increasing inflation by making imports more expensive? In view of the government's political difficulties, would there ever come a point when the government would overrule the Bank of England and refuse a rate rise because of its unpopularity?

By the beginning of May, the pound stood at about 2.20 marks. By any economic standards it seemed ludicrously cheap – unless there was to be a full-blown political crisis ... Then on Thursday 4 May the Conservatives lost catastrophically in the local government elections. There seemed to be no bottom to the electoral pit. On 5 May the Chancellor of the Exchequer, Kenneth Clarke, decided not to increase interest rates, apparently in the face of the Bank of England's preference for a rate rise. That weekend the Sunday papers assumed the worst: this had been a political decision, and when business opened the next week there would be a tidal wave of selling, with scarcely a buyer in sight. Presumed disagreement between the Chancellor and the Bank was the beginning of a nightmare: tactical politics had taken over from sound economic management. Unless there really was evidence that the economy had already started to soften and that another rate rise would be an overdose ...

When trading opened the next week the pound was indeed sold off. It sank below 2.18 – its lowest level ever – on the Tuesday. Where next? Would the government be forced to hike rates simply in order to prevent a rout in the exchange markets, which might bring on a terminal political crisis at Westminster?

At this point events started to go the Chancellor's way. The dollar started to rally sharply against the German mark on the Wednesday – providing, as ever, relief to the beleaguered pound. Buyers began putting their heads over the parapets. Maybe Clarke was right when he claimed that he had made an economic judgement, not a political one. Suddenly, those who had sold rushed to cover their losses. Panic buying of pounds drove the value up from 2.17 to 2.27 – a gain of 4 per cent in just two days. Then the following week, new data on the British economy showed unexpectedly weak consumer sales; so, far from overheating, the momentum of growth was actually fading. The economic data were going Clarke's way after all.

Was all this just a little squall, soon past? The start of a new upswing which would carry the pound back up to the levels of 1994? Or the harbinger of future crises as the government lurched nearer to a general election it clearly did not relish? Clarke had been lucky now, but what about the next time? There were no more sharp moves in May. The sterling market took a breather, but the questions were still there.

2. Was the dollar about to rally?

Since the mid-1980s the dollar had been weakening against the German mark and the Japanese yen. There had been occasional recoveries, most recently a small rally in the latter part of 1994. The weakness had been due to a persistent current account deficit, as well as to relatively low interest rates compared to other countries, particularly in

Europe. But since early 1994 the US monetary authorities had been steadily raising interest rates in order to prevent the economy from overheating, and the trade picture had improved. Surely, therefore, there were no reasons for the dollar to continue sliding in this way? Surely, in fact, it was due for a rally?

Yet since the beginning of 1995 the dollar had slid still more sharply, losing 10 per cent against the mark (and even more gainst the yen) between January and April. This fall was triggered partly by a sudden financial crisis in Mexico – a country inextricably linked economically with the United States through a newly signed free trade agreement – which the markets read as requiring an expensive bail-out by the US government. The currency market remained cautious despite an economy which was in fact growing robustly – more strongly than any of its major competitors – without producing any particularly worrying signs of rising inflation.

Then in April, the US government – which for years had a running argument with Japan about the size of its trade surplus – announced that it would impose punitive tariffs on the import of Japanese luxury cars unless the Japanese agreed to open up their home market more freely to American exports. Did this represent a new US strategy? Rather than waiting for Japanese industry to be stretched on the rack of an ever-rising yen, were the Americans going for more direct action instead? If so, would it achieve results?

After taking a few days to digest the implications, buyers suddenly emerged. Maybe the dollar was oversold? Maybe this was the signal everyone had been awaiting for so long? In a few days, starting on 10 May, the dollar rallied sharply, gaining around 8 per cent from its lows of the previous month (and, as already noted, dragging the pound up with it). Meanwhile there were some signs of Japanese investors showing a trickle of interest in buying American assets. If that trickle became a flood because enough investors believed that the dollar had passed the worst, the rally could become a vertical take-off.

But the rally stalled. A week after it had got under way the stock market – which had almost daily been scaling new heights – fell sharply, losing almost 2 per cent in one day. The reason: company profits were showing unexpected signs of weakness. There were new indicators that the pace of economic growth was slowing, and a slowing economy would lead the authorities to relax interest rates rather than raising them any further. But reducing rates always tends to weaken the currency, as investors shift funds to other currencies with higher rates. Furthermore, the trade dispute with Japan had not, after all, been solved. If it escalated, it was far from clear that this would benefit the US economy. Within a few days the impetus for a dollar rally was gone. The dollar began drifting down again. A lurch downwards on 25 May seemed to presage another major decline.

Then suddenly, on the very last day of the month, the world's central banks, led by the American Federal Reserve, waded in and bought dollars in massive amounts.[2] Their timing was brilliant, striking before the drift became a slide. The sellers were caught completely by surprise. The dollar rose immediately, making back all its losses of the previous few days and ending the month above where it started.

Had the dollar turned, or was this just a temporary reversal in a long-term downward trend? Were the central banks prepared to play the role of King Canute? The signals, as usual, were confusing. The weight of opinion still lay with the pessimists, but sellers were now nervous. The optimists had been saying the dollar was too cheap for so long now, but eventually, like those who predict the end of the world, might they not prove to be right? The only thing the markets felt sure of was that the real rally, if and when it came, would start suddenly – just as this small May rally did.

3. Was this the end of a strong French franc?

The French had been pursuing a '*franc fort*' policy – i.e. a strong franc, tied closely to the German mark – for almost a decade. They had built a politically stable and prosperous country whose affluence and quality of life was the secret envy of their ancient rival across the Channel. And they were determined to partner Germany in leading Europe to an ever-closer union which would banish the ghosts of the past for ever.

But they were paying a price for hitching the franc to the German wagon. Interest rates had to be kept very high and so unemployment was high – 12 per cent, and perhaps double that rate amongst poorer immigrant communities. Social tensions were smouldering, and the lengthy election campaign for a new President to succeed the ageing Francois Mitterand reached its climax in May. In the first round of voting the previous month the far-right, anti-immigrant candidate had polled alarmingly strongly. In the final run-off on 7 May Jacques Chirac was the probable winner – although much less of a racing certainty than he had seemed two months earlier. His central campaign promise was to address the unemployment problem. What did all this mean for the franc?

The markets looked on nervously. Key supporters of Chirac had been known in the past to question the sacred policy of the *franc fort*. Why not devalue, reduce interest rates and let a growing economy mop up the unemployment? In the run-up to the election, the franc had already weakened a fraction and the Paris stock market was racing ahead in anticipation of falling interest rates. On 7 May Chirac edged home. Now what? On the subject of the currency, the new government was loud in its protestations of virtue. There would be no abandonment of the *franc fort*. They would tackle unemployment through government programmes and incentives, paid for by taxes. All would be revealed in a new budget in June. The partnership with Germany and the currency link were sacrosanct. The markets wondered aloud: did they really mean it?

Undoubtedly, there was a huge amount riding on the outcome. If the franc were allowed to drift down against the mark, it would have much wider consequences than just in France. It would put in jeopardy the whole project of European Monetary Union – which would lose all its significance if one of the two major currencies of the Union were to stand aside. There was no doubt that the French government would fight hard to retain the *franc fort*, and would probably get strong support from the German central bank in the process.

The markets were quiet, but far from relaxed. The franc neither strengthened nor weakened in May by more than a fraction, for nothing significant would happen until after the new budget. Then it would become possible to see how the tax and spending numbers would add up, and to estimate the results in terms of employment, inflation and interest rates. But the clouds gathering on the horizon were already visible, particularly in the French government bond market – where bond prices fell, signalling an expectation of higher rates. It was not a good omen for the French government. It was all the more worrisome because every other bond market in the world was booming, as expectations for declining rates in the world at large gathered pace. It looked as if there would be a hot summer in the French markets. But in May an uneasy calm prevailed.

4. Was the world slowing down?

Why were all the other bond markets, apart from France, booming? In 1994, strong growth in several countries – the United States, Britain and Germany, as well as in several newer economies of Asia and Latin America – had caused central monetary authorities to worry that inflation might pick up again as bottlenecks created shortages and led in turn to price rises. Not all the world was enjoying boom conditions: France was not; more importantly, Japan was not. But there was enough concern in the United States to cause the authorities there to raise US interest rates several times during the year, with the result that rates were doubled between the beginning and the end of the year. Rates rose similarly in Britain.

Yet inflation never really took off. Actual inflation seemed to be consistently better than forecast – although the pattern was, as so often, mixed: in early 1995 there were indicators of stronger inflation, particularly in the US economy. So in early 1995, expectations were still for further rate rises in the United States as well as in Britain. Only in Japan – still mired in recession – and in Germany, where the renewed rise of the mark risked causing a slow-down by pricing German exports out of world markets, was there any reason to believe that rates might fall further.

Rising rates are not good for the world's bond markets. If you think rates are going up (and/or if you think inflation is rising) you do not buy fixed-rate bonds. Thus these markets had been very badly hit in 1994, and were still in the doldrums in early 1995. Yet in March and April they began to rally. Why? At the time, there seemed to be no ready explanation for this rally, which had taken many participants by surprise. There was no clear news about the real economies of the world which might have suggested a slow-down. Yet the fact is that as soon as investors think rates have stopped rising, they rush to buy in the bond market, to lock in high returns whilst rates are at their peak before they start falling again. This is what had begun to happen. In other words, expectations had shifted.

And the market's instinct was right, because in May the evidence started to trickle through. Statistics on manu-facturing investment in the United States and on consumer behaviour in Britain started to paint a picture of weakening demand. Critical voices began to be heard: the monetary authorities had tightened the noose too hard. Before long, some argued, there might even be a slump if conditions were not relaxed. As we have seen, a bout of nerves struck the US stock market, which noted the slightly weaker level of corporate profits and began to wonder if this was the harbinger of a serious downturn. Meanwhile, the bond markets took further encouragement (for a downturn is *good* news for the bond markets) and climbed further.

Not that everything suddenly pointed one way – that is almost never the case. There were plenty of investors who anticipated that any slow-down would be only mild and temporary, lasting perhaps for three or six months. If so, those who were rushing to buy bonds might well get caught out later in the year. And in any case, the bond markets had moved so sharply already that it was far from clear how much further they could go, even if the fore-casters of a slow-down were wholly right.

The evidence, as ever, was mixed. The authorities had to decide whether to continue with the recent policy of gradually ratcheting rates upward, or whether to hold, or even cut them. The bond market had to decide whether to buy further, or whether prices had already moved far enough in anticipation of a slow-down. The stock market had to decide how far a slow-down would impact corporate profits, and how quickly. And the currency markets had to decide which economies would be affected most – leading to the sharpest reductions in rates, and thus to relatively weaker currencies. The connectedness of the markets was never more obvious.

* * *

So the pound did not crash; the dollar did not rally; the French franc was nervous; and, as to whether the world was slowing down, it would be months before the picture was clear. Put like that, it sounds as though nothing much happened. But market-making carried on day in, day out, pushed and pulled by expectations and the occasional piece of hard economic evidence. All of which goes to show that nothing is certain. For governments charged with managing monetary policy, the experience is like driving a car with no front windscreen and only a rear-view mirror for guidance. For the general public in Britain, the main result in May 1995 was that mortgage rates did not go up, but house prices were falling again; and holiday costs started to bear the brunt of the weaker pound.

By the end of 1995 some things had become clearer. The dollar had rallied significantly. The pound was stable. The French franc had proven remarkably firm, although the markets were still watching closely. And the world's economy had slowed down somewhat, but not as much as many had feared.

But the story never finishes. Like an unending soap opera, there are always new episodes to come. Some characters retire and are written out of the script; others take their place. New sub-plots develop: some become major themes, whilst others evaporate like morning mist. New dénouements occur, but they are never the final word. For the markets are not like individual human lives, which have an ending; they are a microcosm of the flow of human affairs as a whole, which does not.

The only thing we know for sure is that it is not possible to legislate away the uncertainty. There is no Great Planner anywhere who can tell governments, banks, traders, or the general public what the 'right' level of interest rates should be or what the 'right' value of currencies should be. The belief in a rational solution dies hard, perhaps – the idea that there must surely be a set of mathematical equations detailed and complex enough, and a computer large enough to solve them, so that humanity could do away with the shifting volatility of the markets once and for all. But there is no such certainty to be had. In that sense, the markets are simply a reminder of a wider truth about human experience. We live with ambiguity and insecurity. To the humdrum questions of human commerce we find an uncertain and purely provisional answer through the serendipity of the markets, just as we find an uncertain and provisional way through the happenstances of life itself. There is no other way.

NOTES

1 If the dollar weakens, investors take cover in the two great 'hard' currencies of the world – the German mark and the Japanese yen. This pushes up the value of the mark (and of the yen) and so normally means that the mark rises against other currencies, such as sterling, as well. Conversely, when the dollar strengthens, the pound typically strengthens against the mark.

2 Central banks occasionally intervene in the currency markets, though often with only limited and very transient results. They do so, typically, to 'smooth' markets which they view as moving too far too fast, rather than to alter a fundamental trend. They have considerable fire-power, but not enough to turn a trend for very long.

4

The Market: Servant or Master?

The evidence of the last chapter is not enough to prove that an alternative to the markets is unrealistic in our world today. It is not sufficient to show that we cannot force the variables of the market into some grand plan which would remove the volatility and the uncertainty. We still have to deal with the charge that the financial markets are incompatible with the Christian law of love. How can it ever be argued that the noisy, competitive greed of the market can promote human welfare and the kingdom of God? Some will say that it is – or can be – a means to that end. Yet the whole point of the story of Jesus' temptations in the wilderness is that the end does not justify the means: if you choose the wrong means, you do not get to the right end. Not even the Son of God could compel people to accept the kingdom of God, and he refused to jump through the hoops set by the devil. One cannot turn stones into bread or be the servant of evil – not even for the kingdom of God. The prophets of the market claim that it is an efficient means of providing bread for humanity. But we do not live by bread alone ...

In any case, how good *is* the market at providing bread for humanity? It is obvious that not enough bread is available in the world. The sight of children with swollen bellies and dull eyes is a standing indictment of humanity. Whilst this happens, the world is out of joint and the kingdom of God is disgraced. The market, to justify its existence, has to show – directly, or at least indirectly – that it enables more of the human necessities for life to be produced and distributed to those who need them, not just to those who already have an abundance of everything and yet still feel in want. Trading money has to produce bread for the hungry.

Yet the tragedy is that the countries where bread is scarce are ones which are virtually excluded from the world's financial markets. Africa, which is home to more such countries than any other continent, is like the dog that did not bark. A survey of the global markets would show just how small a ripple Africa makes. Africa contains thirty-three of the forty-eight countries which make up the United Nations' list of least developed countries. The whole continent, apart from South Africa, went almost unmentioned in the *Financial Times* during May 1995. In fact, it often goes virtually unmentioned from one month to the next. When it is eventually mentioned, it is all too often to report failure. Yet one in eight of the world's population lives there, crushed under the legacy of colonial fragmentation and mismanagement (in some cases), and present mismanagement (in all too many cases). These countries play little part in the international markets. They raise virtually no capital in the international bond markets and receive only about 1 per cent of international direct investment. Viewed from the perspective of poor African countries, many of which are in a worse condition now than they were a generation ago, the international financial system is a distant irrelevance. In some cases, it is the channel for a crushing burden of debt repayments on past loans which have been mismanaged or misappropriated by corrupt leaders.

The statistics are bleak: Life expectancy in much of Africa is less than fifty, and has been falling in many areas. Millions have died of starvation. Political instability is widespread and several countries have experienced years of civil war. Average incomes may have fallen by as much as a quarter in the 1980s. More generally, the poorest countries of the world still seem to be losing ground. In the 1990s their annual growth rate of output averaged 1.5 per cent. Since their populations have been growing at almost double that rate, this means that average incomes are still declining. They are caught in a vice, as their staple agricultural output has failed to keep pace with population growth whilst their share of world agricultural exports has halved since 1980. As a 1995 United Nations report warns:

> *Without the benefit of sustained*
> *international support, the least developed*
> *countries will most probably become*
> *further marginalized as the process of*
> *globalization gains further momentum.*[1]

Yet anyone who can recall the zeal with which the cause of overseas aid was taken up in Western countries in the

1960s – by the public as well as the private sectors – cannot help but be aware of the fatigue and loss of confidence which has overtaken the whole enterprise in recent years. For the last twenty years, the rich countries have provided only about a third of 1 per cent of their gross national product in government aid to developing countries. And there seems to be little or no political will to increase that share.

This is a human disaster of quite phenomenal proportions. It has been as expensive in human lives as if there had been a major war. Yet because such bleak evidence has been drip-fed into the media over the years (and because it is not on the doorstep of the rich), it has arguably caused the rich world less anguish than the break-up of Yugoslavia. The challenge to Christians who listen for the voice of God is clear. We cannot rest easy and not hear.

But the question is, does this tragedy demand that humanity abandon the use of markets in order to respond effectively to this challenge? The answer is surely, no. There are certainly many defects in the working of the markets, particularly the distortions which impede poor countries from exporting agricultural and other low-technology goods to the rich countries. And there are many things wrong with the management of poor countries which have caused opportunities to be squandered. But government planning approaches imported from Western countries in the 1960s and – all too often – the way in which foreign aid has been used have combined to stifle commercial initiative and economic growth. It requires a dedicated refusal to look reality in the face to assert, in the light of the last thirty years, that what such countries need is less of the market and more planning and regulation.

But what if the workings of the markets have been such that, in practice, the poor are forced to participate on terms which would be considered so iniquitous in a wealthy country that they would be outside the law? Sweat-shops in many parts of Africa, Asia and Latin America employ workers in conditions which would be illegal in any European country. Often, cheap labour is used on terms not far from literal slavery. In all too many cases children are employed, working long hours from early years in often appalling conditions. Is this due to the fact that importers from the wealthy countries are in a monopoly bargaining position? Sometimes, maybe, but they are not generally monopolists in their home markets, which are ruthlessly competitive. No, the real reason for these employment conditions is simply that labour is cheap and plentiful in poor countries – a fact which both they and the rich-country importers know. This is the savage reality which lies behind all the dry textbook language about markets and the laws of supply and demand.

The Christian conscience cries out that this is wrong – that human beings are being sacrificed for the consumer paradises of the rich world. But what to do? The difficulty of preventing abuse is highlighted by the issue of child labour, which jogs the consciences of the rich world particularly strongly. Take the case of the textile industry of Bangladesh, which in recent years has had increasing success in exporting to the North American market. The use of child labour was widespread until pressure on American importers not to allow children to be used in the manufacture of products bought by them resulted in up to 30,000 children losing their jobs. A study by Oxfam found that many ended up not in school, but in welding shops (much more dangerous than textiles) or even in prostitution.[2]

So is there any better way? The prophets of the market say that there is no simple answer, and none at all which does not involve retaining market involvement and competitiveness. It will not help the poor if the rich stop buying clothes made in the developing countries. Nor will crude interference designed to alter the supply and demand equation. What if, for example, the labour cost is only one-hundredth of the final price to the consumer in London or Paris? Could not wages be doubled without the consumer noticing? Yet no one can avoid the impersonal competitive pressures which will ensure that the importers look for the cheapest supply. So raising the price of labour artificially in one country risks causing the importers to go elsewhere for a cheaper source of labour. And, as the above case study shows, even the attempt to ban child labour can all too easily backfire. What is needed, says the market textbook, is not some artificial means of raising wages – which will either fail or result in fewer people being employed – but more free trade so that the developing countries can sell more produce and so increase their national income. What is needed, in other words, is *more* market – not less.

But however much the market may seem to be necessary, says the voice of protest, it is certainly not suffi- cient. To rely solely on the slow process of market activity to raise the standard of living to acceptable levels is to condemn both the present generation and the next – and perhaps the one after that – to a short life of grinding hardship. There is surely no need to wait this long. The Europeans of today enjoy an affluence so large that from the point of view of an African it must seem as though every one of them had won the lottery. Yet these modern Europeans stand on the shoulders of forgotten armies of Victorian workers who slaved away and died in the mines and the factories of grim industrial cities. Perhaps this was largely inevitable; in the nineteenth century there was not enough surplus wealth to fund development, and technology was far cruder than today. So economic progress had to inch forward on the back of grinding hard work. But in the twentieth century there must surely be a better way.

For there is nothing inevitable nowadays about sacrificing generations of developing-country workers so that future ones can enjoy a tolerable standard of living. The world has enough technology and wealth to give a reasonable standard of living to everyone in this generation. What it needs, says the voice of protest, is not just the slow, hard process of poor countries trading their way out of misery, but a real transfer of purchasing power from the rich to the poor. This will never be achieved simply by relying on the forces of the markets. As we have seen, the poorest countries cannot even borrow in the world's markets, let alone achieve a real shift in the ownership of capital.

The results of such a transfer could unquestionably be dramatic if the amounts were large enough. The forced transfer of wealth from the rich countries to the Middle Eastern oil exporters in the 1970s and 1980s is an example of what can happen. After the oil shocks of the 1970s, which dramatically increased the price of oil, the annual cash flow to the Gulf oil producers reached $200 billion in 1980 (compared with total overseas aid in the same year of only $6 billion). These massive inflows of finance permitted the complete transformation of those societies from hard desert livelihoods to widespread affluence in less than twenty years. There is no reason to believe that the same results could not be achieved by similar transfers elsewhere. There is in fact nothing inevitable, so the voice of a twentieth-century Amos would say, about poverty and under-development.

Maybe, say the defenders of the market, but the population of Africa is a hundred times the population of Saudi Arabia, and the transfer of wealth to the oil producers was not a voluntary act of altruism. The history of overseas aid (the only significant unforced transfer of purchasing power to poor countries) hardly encourages any hope for a quantum leap to the levels of financial transfer enjoyed by the Middle Eastern oil exporters. In practice, the world cannot afford to wait for an attack of such generosity to overcome the rich. Free trade and free markets are the only realistic way of escaping from poverty.

What is more, there are a growing number of countries in Asia and elsewhere which show how competitive performance in the international markets can bring big dividends. Hong Kong, Singapore, Malaysia, China, Thailand and others have enjoyed rapid growth rates through active participation in the world's trading markets. In Hong Kong in the 1950s people died in their thousands from cholera; now it has an average income per head which is higher than that of Britain. Malaysia has enjoyed economic growth of at least 8 per cent for the last few years (compared with an average of about 2 per cent in Britain). Such a performance has the effect of doubling national income every eight years or so. In fact, the economic transformation of Asia as a whole is clearly the most momentous change the world has seen in this generation, apart from the collapse of world communism. And that change has been wholly oriented towards the international markets.

It would, of course, be simplistic to ignore the other factors involved in Asia's success. Except perhaps in the case of Hong Kong, these countries are not pure textbook examples of free trading and free financial markets.[3] They are also the beneficiaries of cultures which have supported a high level of social cohesion and high literacy rates. So facile comparisons with other markets should not be drawn. And yet they are surely a beacon of hope in an otherwise uncertain outlook.

Poorer countries have, in practice, no alternative but to look to the market for growth. The experience of central planning, whether Soviet-style or the kind sponsored by Western academics in the 1960s, has shown that it will not rescue them from hunger. And the political will amongst the wealthy countries to help them achieve rapid development through major financial transfers is clearly limited. The market is their only real hope. In any event, even if the world were, miraculously, to agree on a massive redistribution of capital so as to permit rapid transformation of the poorest countries, it would still need the market to allocate that capital to the most productive investments, to achieve lasting growth and put an end for ever to the scarcity of bread. The market may indeed not be sufficient, but it is surely necessary. Its results are not perfect, but it can be a good servant.

But, on the contrary, the market is *not* a good servant, cries the voice of protest. In fact, it is an impersonal, unbending master. The poor know that the financial markets show no mercy in their punishment of those who stumble. Mexico found this out in late 1994. It had been enjoying strong growth and relatively prudent government budget policies, but internal political tensions – fuelled in part by regional insurrection against the central government – together with a dangerously high level of borrowing from foreign sources led suddenly to a financial crisis. This forced the currency to devalue and caused the stock market to drop like a stone as panicking investors sold out of their holdings. The lesson seemed to be clear: governments as well as individual companies had to be careful how they managed their exposure to lenders and investors through the markets. Otherwise, they risked discovering that the transition from favourite son to prodigal son is lightning-fast.

Furthermore, it is not just the poor who have to bow to market power. Rich countries, too, experience the merciless logic of the markets, sometimes at the expense of the policies of democratically elected governments. Take, for example, the case of Britain's experience with the European Exchange Rate Mechanism (ERM). For several years, up to 1992, the government sought to follow a policy of keeping the pound within the ERM. This meant maintaining interest rates at a level which ensured that the pound's exchange rate remained effectively linked tightly to the German mark. But in 1992 the mark was strengthening and huge market pressure was building up against the pound.[4] Would the government be able, politically, to get away with putting up interest rates to whatever level was necessary to deter sellers and attract buyers? Eventually, in September 1992, the crisis burst. The Bank of England intervened repeatedly in the market, supporting the currency by buying pounds at the ERM rate. But the weight of selling pressure behind the dam was now too great, and in one night, on Wednesday 16 September (immediately dubbed Black Wednesday by the media), the dam gave way. The government put up interest rates from 10 to 12 per cent – and then to 15 per cent – as the selling of the pound continued unabated through the day. But even this penal rate failed to deter the sellers since no one was convinced that the government would be able to hold the rate for long, let alone raise it further if needed. The economy was already in a serious condition: companies were failing, unemployment was rising and house prices were falling even before these emergency rate hikes. Late in the evening the government gave up. It cancelled the last rate rise and the pound was allowed to slide. It lost 5 per cent against the mark in the next 24 hours. The pound was out of the ERM.[5]

Was this an example of an unwarranted defeat for democracy by the impersonal and unaccountable forces of the market? To some it felt so at the time. But others noted that this defeat ushered in a period of new growth for the British economy which enabled it to surge out of recession, ahead of the rest of Europe. One financial journalist caught this new mood of relief and freedom by renaming 16 September White Wednesday – the day when the British economy was freed from the rack and the government regained control of its destiny. Looking back on that September day, it did not feel at all as if the markets had been guilty of undemocratic abuse of power; rather, they had simply shown that the emperor had no clothes.

In fact, it could be argued that the market, far from being a faceless force uncontrolled by any democratic accountability, has an intuitive sense of what public opinion will and will not tolerate, which is far more acute than that of all too many politicians. Ironically, in view of its reputation for being focused on nothing longer term than the next five minutes, the market also has an acute nose for longer-term problems cumulating over the horizon. Like cattle that gather beneath the trees long before the rain actually comes, the market can feel trouble in the atmosphere. The events of September 1992 in Britain demonstrate that the markets understood clearly enough the unwillingness of the British public to endure the level of interest rates and the depth of recession which would have been needed to reinforce a link of the pound with the German mark.

But the trouble with the markets as a democratic force, the cynic might say, is that the wrong sorts of people get the vote. The British government in 1992 and the Mexican government in 1994 both had unpleasant rebuffs delivered from the tribune of the market-place. In both cases there were many foreigners casting their ballots. The faceless international fund managers turned their thumbs down on the pound and the Mexican peso. This may not raise major moral issues in the case of Britain, particularly since their actions came to be widely regarded as having done the country a favour. But what about a poor, struggling economy like Mexico, desperately short of capital and punished because it borrowed too much from foreigners?[6] If this was democracy, maybe Mexico needed something better.

But what, exactly? The Mexican government learnt the need for a more robust financing policy. In addition, the Mexican experience sent a shock, which inevitably became known as the 'Mexican wave', through the financial markets. Some of the so-called 'emerging markets countries'[7] were largely unscathed because they had much more manageable and carefully structured borrowing programmes. Others, whose monetary position resembled that of Mexico, had to reassess their exposure to the markets in the light of this experience. The end result may have been the adoption of sounder, and therefore more durable, borrowing and lending policies generally in emerging markets finance.

In the end, the case for the markets is not unlike the case for democracy itself, as famously articulated by Churchill. The markets are by no means a perfect way of allocating capital; it is just that any alternative is worse. Christian writers have often been loath to accept this fact. They are apt to lament the gross inequalities of the world and to demand that they be wished away by means more direct than the markets appear to offer. It is undoubtedly true that the markets cannot function effectively for human development on their own. It is clear, for example, that the progress which has been made in recent years in alleviating the Third World debt crisis could not have been achieved without government involvement (notably through the so-called Brady scheme).[8] And special measures going beyond anything that the international markets could provide spontaneously will certainly be necessary to deal with the plight of the poorest countries. But it is hard indeed to see how the market can be dispensed with as a servant of economic growth, whether or not we entirely trust it.

And there is no need to be too trusting. The world's greatest economists have been all too aware of the dangers inherent in the markets – the dangers, for instance, of cartels, or of erratic speculation. Adam Smith himself was in no way naïve about the markets and the motives of those who participate:

> People of the same trade seldom meet
> together even for merriment or diversion,
> but the conversation ends in a conspiracy
> against the public, or in some contrivance
> to raise prices.[9]

John Maynard Keynes, the great economist who had immense influence on government economic policy in the wake of the world depression of the 1930s (and who was himself an extremely shrewd investor in the markets), well understood what happens to an economy when feverish speculation takes over from real investment:

> Speculators may do no harm as bubbles on
> a steady stream of enterprise. The position

> *is serious when enterprise becomes the*
> *bubble on a whirlpool of speculation. When*
> *the capital development of a country is the*
> *by-product of the activities of a casino, the*
> *job is likely to be ill done.*[10]

Whatever else they said, these two economists had in common a conviction that the markets need to be watched to make sure that they remain good servants of economic growth.

At this point, however, the angry voice of the modern prophet cries out that economic growth is precisely what the human race cannot afford much more of. It is precisely because the market is focused on – not to say obsessed with – economic growth that it is not our servant: it has become a Frankenstein we cannot control. For the world faces limits. We surely cannot continue indefinitely to expand our consumption of the earth's resources – even its so-called renewable ones, let alone those that are finite or renewable only over hundreds of millions of years. We cannot afford to pour even more pollutants and gases into the atmosphere as the world's economies grow ever more hungry for energy. Adam and Eve were told to be fruitful and to subdue the earth; we are in danger of rendering it barren. If the market fuels growth, we cannot afford it much longer.

Yet we do not know exactly where the limits are. They may well be imprecise and shifting. The influential book *The Limits to Growth*, published over twenty years ago, forecast that food and industrial output per head would begin to collapse, under the impact of exploding population growth, soon after the millennium.[11] But detailed forecasting of the limits to growth is an uncertain art. Perhaps the *Limits to Growth* team did not envisage just how rapidly many economies, particularly in Asia, would have grown by then. Yet it is a cheap response to dismiss the whole topic by assuming that technological progress will always act as a *Deus ex machina*, and by noting that horse-drawn vehicles were once at risk of bringing London to a standstill because of the geometrically rising output of manure. No one can be confident that the human race will succeed on present trends in avoiding the consequences of raping and pillaging the earth the way we have done. We clearly have to recognize that there is an impending crisis – which the present generation will probably not face, but which may well burst on our grandchildren.

So as the crisis looms, environmentalists demand co-ordinated action on many fronts: reduced consumption by the rich, control of deforestation, more support for population policies, investment which is environmentally compatible, better waste management, etc. We can hardly afford, many will say, to rely on market forces to achieve all this. We have to stop treating progress as just a matter of more and more economic growth. Unless we can achieve a co-operation which goes beyond ruthless market competition, we have little hope.

But if we could not make use of the markets, then, on past performance, we would indeed have little hope. The record of human collaboration is patchy at best, even when the benefits are obvious and immediate. When the reason is to avoid a future catastrophe whose exact nature or timing we cannot predict and which may not occur with full force during the lives of anyone presently living, then the prospects for comprehensive co-operation of the kind the most passionate environmentalists call for are slim indeed. The question of the future habitability of the planet is both serious and complex, and well beyond the scope of this book. But what is certain is that for as long as human nature remains as it is, any initiatives for a better environment will need to work with and through the market if they are to be effective.

Indeed, some of the more fanatical prophets of the market have been known to argue that the workings of the market are sufficient in themselves to ensure avoidance of disaster. Scarcity provokes price rises, which reduce demand. But this magical theorem does not save species from extinction when the price of a rhino's horn is a king's ransom for a poacher but a small item on the bank account of a wealthy Asian magnate. Nor does it prevent pollutants being poured out into the atmosphere when the costs are borne by others, not by the polluter. It would be foolish to rely solely on the laws of supply and demand. The human race needs all the painfully slow, imperfect and grudging co-operation it can muster to save its whales, its Siberian tigers, its rain forests, its atmosphere and the future of its children.

The fact remains, however, that the market is an incredibly effective method of translating consumer consciousness, and indeed public policy objectives, into demand and supply responses. The US economy, for example, is the largest consumer of energy per person of any major country. Why? Because energy is cheaper there than in any other major country. A significant tax on petrol, as in Europe, would rapidly encourage the substitution of smaller cars for larger ones, with attendant benefits for the environment (as well as for the government's fiscal position). The cost of properly disposing of old cars could be included, by government regulation, in the purchase price of new cars. Effective pricing for road usage, which may at last become possible using modern electronic tracking methods, would encourage greater rationing of private cars and more use of environmentally acceptable public transport. And so on. The opportunities are legion.

The market also remains an outstandingly powerful mechanism for evolving technical progress, which will surely be needed in the fight for the future. The most important example of this is certainly the information revolution, whose impact on the entire structure of economies – indeed on human consciousness itself – may yet turn out to be the most crucial legacy of the twentieth century. It is hard to imagine any other mechanism than the market which would have spread its capabilities so far and so fast throughout the world.

All in all, the conclusion must surely be that the market can indeed be harnessed for the kingdom of God. To go back to where this chapter started, the market *can* provide bread for humanity, both now and in the future, and provide it efficiently too. That real markets do not often work well enough to do so is due to their imperfections and misuse, not to any intrinsic evil in them. It must certainly be acknowledged that, left to their own devices, real markets are unlikely to distribute wealth effectively in accordance with the Christian imperative, or to ensure that the resources of the earth are properly tended. But properly used, the power of the market can be harnessed for good.

Many people instinctively want to reach for a more black-and-white conclusion than this. They want a ringing endorsement of the power of the markets; or they want them condemned as hopelessly distorted and oppressive in their effects. But the truth warrants neither of these clear-cut judgements. What we can say is that the prevalent climate of opinion in the first two or three decades after the Second World War was unduly suspicious of the markets as an engine of development. Since then the balance has shifted towards a much clearer recognition of their value, and of the bankruptcy of development approaches which do not allow them a central and pervasive role in economic activity. The markets as we know them are obviously imperfect – that much is clear whilst whole peoples are excluded from the bounty of the planet. But there is no alternative than to make active use of this effective servant, despite the misgivings of many. Other ways have been tried and have failed. We may wish things were otherwise, but they are not.

* * *

The striking fact about all this is that it is exactly what the Christian insight into the kingdom of God should lead us to expect. What, after all, *is* the kingdom of God? It is precisely the state of affairs in which God's sovereignty is recognized and accepted as creative and redeeming love by humanity at large. The Christian understanding is that *this sovereignty has been inaugurated through Jesus Christ, is growing in our midst, and will be fully consummated as human history comes to a climax.* We live between the times, so to speak: still our old selves, that we know so well; yet called to live in the light of a promised transformation – which is not only possible, but eventually will be complete. This basic insight of Christian faith has two important implications for a Christian view of markets as a human institution.

First, it proclaims that human history and development has an end-point, a climax to which it is moving. Human experience is neither an endlessly repeating cycle nor a morass from which individuals are plucked out here and there for salvation. The promise is of a transformation, the exact nature of which is so hard to predict or to envisage that those who speak of it fall naturally into poetry as the only means of describing it:

> The wolf shall live with the lamb,
>> the leopard shall lie down with the kid,
> the calf and the lion and the fatling together,
>> and a little child shall lead them.
> The cow and the bear shall graze,
>> their young shall lie down together;
>> and the lion shall eat straw like the ox ...
> They shall not hurt or destroy
>> on all my holy mountain;
> for the earth will be full of the knowledge of the Lord
>> as the waters cover the sea.
> (Isaiah 11:6–9)

This is poetry, groping at images to convey the wonder of a transformed life beyond the horizons of our patchy experience. Elsewhere, and more directly imaginable, Old

Testament prophets look to a time when

> *they shall beat their swords into ploughshares,*
> *and their spears into pruning hooks;*
> *nation shall not lift up sword against nation*
> *neither shall they learn war anymore ...*
> (Micah 4:3)

It may be tempting to dismiss all this as pure fantasy, far removed from anything we know. But its real purpose is to remind us of how much we should long for a fulfilment to human history which will be far better than the present reality. The vivid pictures of a reality so transformed that ancient natural enmities are resolved into harmony are a parable of the kingdom of God in all its fullness. With that as our vision, we are called never to be content with the status quo, never to be complacent. We must not treat the present reality of what we do as the be-all and end-all, and that applies with full force to the business of the markets.

Secondly, we live in the meantime in a sort of half-way house, with one foot in the world as it is and one in the kingdom of God. We have a vision of the end-point, but we live in the real world of the present, with all its existing imperfect structures and technologies. Our calling is to live out the Christian life in that historical interim, without pretending that we can leap straight to the end-point, and to work for the advancement of the kingdom. We are called to live with the human nature and the mechanisms of the world as it is, and to work with them – without either glorifying the status quo or denying its existence. We are called neither to lose the vision nor to deny the facts of life. That means, in particular, that we need to be prepared to work with something as provisional but as effective as the markets – which take humans as they are, and yet can be used to help create something they yearn for.

It is clear from Jesus' teaching what this involves. Several of the key principles underlying the body of his teaching bear on this need to live and work in the interim with the markets. First, there is the absolute priority he accords to the kingdom of God. More than all else – more even than worrying about the basic issues of food and clothing, more certainly than worrying about riches and culture – we are to strive *first* for the kingdom of God and his righteousness (see Matthew 6:33). As Christians, in short, we are called to look beyond the immediate to the ultimate. We do what we do because it advances the kingdom.

However, lest we fall into the trap of misusing that principle to dismiss concerns about poverty in the world (on the grounds that others should not be worrying about the basics of life either), then a second key principle of Jesus' teaching reminds us that we must love our neighbour as ourselves. And who is our neighbour? The question was asked and received an answer which is arguably the most famous parable of them all: the good Samaritan is neighbour to the beaten victim, even though he comes from a region regarded as foreign and hostile (see Luke 10:29–37). We cannot rule out any part of the human race as being outside our sphere of responsibility. If a child is forced to work in virtual slavery so that we can wear cheap shirts, this must be on our consciences. No one is an island in the global market and no one is an island in the kingdom of God either.

Moreover, Jesus clearly expects his followers to *use* the provisional structures of the present day. As we already noted in Chapter 2, he gives no sign of any disapproval of commercial or financial activity in themselves. He regularly uses parables drawn from everyday commercial life. Whilst he expects people to be transformed in their behaviour, he does not generally call them *out* of their workaday world. Zacchaeus, the ancient world's most famous tax collector (and thus about as popular a figure as the modern City trader), is certainly moved to make amends for dishonesty and to change his ways. Yet Jesus does not call him to give up his profession (see Luke 19:1–10).

All of this has personal implications for those who actually work in the markets, as we shall see. But so far as the market system itself is concerned, it means that if – as is beyond any reasonable doubt – the markets are a necessary part of present life, then Christians are surely called to be there. That being the case, we have to go on to look more closely at the strains and stress of life in that world, which the Church has historically known too little about, as a basis for identifying what Jesus' teaching means for Christian ethics and behaviour in the markets.

NOTES

1 See UNCTAD, *The Least Developed Countries: 1995 Report and Mid-Term Review of the Programme of Action* (New York, 1995).

2 See the article on 'Consciences and Consequences' in *The Economist*, 3 June 1995.

3 In particular, they have in some cases regulated their financial

markets relatively tightly, allowing free convertibility of their currencies but making it difficult for foreigners to buy financial assets. Foreigners are welcomed as direct investors in productive enterprise, but not as short-term speculators in financial assets. Even in the case of the supposedly pure free market of Hong Kong, there has been extensive provision of low-cost public sector housing.

4   German interest rates were rising because of the huge costs of reunification. British interest rates needed to fall because the country was in a deepening recession. These two forces created enormous pressure for the pound to weaken against the mark.

5   The publishing executive responsible for this book vividly remembers these events. He was due to complete buying a house the next day and had taken on the maximum mortgage he could afford. He clearly recalls the rising panic he felt as he heard first one, and then a second increase in rates being announced. Numb with fear, he sat through a day's worth of business meetings, totally unable to concentrate. Then came the news that it was all over. He almost wept for joy.

6   Too much of Mexico's borrowing was short-term – putting the country at risk of a crisis because of the constant need to roll the debt over.

7   This term has become a favourite way of describing those developing countries which are market-oriented, growing rapidly and beginning to be able to access the world's financial markets more readily. Unfortunately, there are still plenty of countries – particularly in Africa – which do not fit this pattern.

8   This scheme, the brain-child of James Brady, US Treasury Secretary under President George Bush, involved substituting secured, marketable bonds for the original loans. The banks which were owed the money gained security and liquidity in return for an element of debt forgiveness. The borrowers were freed from the paralysing burden of unsustainable interest payments.

9 Adam Smith, *The Wealth of Nations*, book I, ch. 10.

10 John Maynard Keynes, *The General Theory of Employment, Interest and Money*, ch. 12.

11 D. Meadows et al., *The Limits to Growth* (London: Pan Books, 1974).

5

Traders: Masters or Servants?

Sherman McCoy, 'master of the universe', top bond salesman at the prestigious Wall Street trading house of Pearce & Pearce, is the hero – and ultimately the victim – in Tom Wolfe's best-selling satirical novel *The Bonfire of the Vanities*. The 'master of the universe', with the power to move mountains and markets, has all the right trappings: the Park Avenue apartment, the summer house at the fashionable end of Long Island, the expensive Mercedes-Benz. But the god is brought down from his Olympian heights in a nightmarish story involving a fatal combination of sex, a driving accident and ward politics. Like all the best satire, the plot of *The Bonfire of the Vanities* is partly preposterous and yet also very near the bone in its portrayal of the lifestyles, the motives and the stresses of its victims. All satire exaggerates, but it starts with acute observation. Tom Wolfe's hero is certainly larger than life, but he is also a challenge because he poses in stark form the question about the *spiritual* effect of the markets on those who play in them.

In Chapter 1, we raised two questions: Do the markets contribute to the kingdom Of God? And what do they do to the spiritual condition of those who are involved in them? In Chapter 4 we faced the first of those two questions; now we must face the second. How can ruthless competition be reconciled with the Christian imperative to love one another? How can the players avoid being corrupted by the materialism and the drive for power and wealth? How can the whole ethos of the markets be considered compatible with Christ's promise that the meek will inherit the earth?

Sherman McCoy is not, of course, the only fictional hero/villain/victim of the financial world. The markets and their raw power-play have inevitably attracted the attention of other writers and film-makers – although the result has often been thoroughly romanticized and sentimental-ized (see, for example, *Working Girl* for the essential Hollywood view of Wall Street – in which girl gets boy, and good triumphs reassuringly over evil). By far the best film view of the markets in recent years was Oliver Stone's 1987 *Wall Street*. In this film a naïve young stockbroker, anxious to make his fortune, becomes the protégé of a seasoned and corrupt Wall Street operator and is seduced into crim-inal dealings by the excitement and the prospect of wealth and power. Gordon Gekko, the obsessive villain of *Wall Street*, sums up the ethos, especially of the 1980s – the heyday of the asset-strippers who bought, sold and dismembered whole companies for a quick profit in the tens of millions. As he tells the shareholders of one of his victims, in a speech which is an apologia for the asset-stripper:

> *... greed is good. Greed is right. Greed*
> *works. Greed clarifies, cuts through and*
> *captures the essence of the evolutionary*
> *spirit. Greed in all its forms – greed for life,*
> *for money, for love, for knowledge – has*
> *marked the upward surge of mankind ...*

Interestingly, there are no comparably successful novels or films set in the City of London.[1] But in the last century Anthony Trollope (best known for his penetrating stories of ecclesiastical life and politics) produced a withering satire of British commercial and financial life in *The Way We Live Now*. Dated though it is in many ways, this novel neverthe-less shows that today's manipulators have their forbears and that greed is as durable as gold. The figure of Augustus Melmotte, Trollope's oily villain who is good at making rich fools part with their money and whose star rises high in the London firmament until it suddenly explodes, could easily have his counterpart in any novel of the present-day City of London.

But it is not only fiction that can seem larger than life. Authors have often lamented the fact that fiction and satire are constantly in danger of being upstaged by reality. And so it has often seemed in the frothy 1980s, and even in the slightly more sober 1990s. Michael Lewis' book *Liar's Poker*, which tells the story of the Wall Street bond trading house of Salomon Brothers, opens with a famous anecdote of the day when the Chairman of the firm publicly challenged one of his senior partners to a round of liar's poker (in which the bluffing and guessing focused on the serial numbers on randomly chosen dollar bills rather than on ordinary playing cards) for a stake of $1 million. The partner raises the ante to $10 million, at which point even the multi-millionaire Chairman backs off.[2]

Nor are the excesses confined to a few legendary episodes like this one. The image of the financial markets – born in the 1980s, and not without foundation even in the more restrained 1990s – has been one of widespread individual and corporate extravagance. The markets created stars, prima donnas whose temperamental behaviour, legendary wealth and exotic lives became the raw material for countless voyeuristic magazine articles. Oh, the art collections, the châteaux, the cars and yachts – and the private lives! This was as good as anything even Hollywood could produce. Nevertheless, it is easy to exaggerate. Though the City of London, like Wall Street, has its characters, both places are filled mainly with people who lead routine, undramatic lives. There are those who spend outrageously and live flamboyantly, but the reality is (mostly) more humdrum. These are not the poor of the earth, obviously; but few live the totally absorbed, obsessive and restless life of a Gekko. Even fewer live the sort of deliberately showy life which attracts the attention of the society magazines.

In any case, it is important not to lose sight of the good things about life in the markets: the energy, the sense of the possible, the scorn for outmoded tradition. At its best, the world of the markets is meritocratic, egalitarian and cosmopolitan. In fact, it is part of the mystique of the modern markets that they provide a way to riches and power for those not born with either. Gekko's defence of himself focuses on the fact that he is the small-town boy made good, who has had to fight every inch of the way, and who has learnt that it is more important to win than to play by the rules. But his is the corrupt version. There are plenty of examples of those who have done well despite having no social or family advantages – and have done so within the rules and by sheer ability and drive.

Nevertheless, there are acute pressures – pressures to compete, pressures to strive for power, pressures to amass wealth. These pressures are not, of course, unique to the City. Anyone with experience of life in large modern corporations knows about both the external and the internal competitive pressures. Externally, the corporation is engaged in a perpetual struggle for markets; internally, the politics of the struggle for the top jobs can be blatant or subtle, but they are almost never absent. In one sense, the City is no different. It too is competitive, both externally and internally. The institutions struggle for market share; individuals struggle for positions of power and influence. Manoeuvring and intrigue are part of commercial life anywhere (and indeed they are not wholly absent from other organizations, even Christian churches!).

Yet the pressures are in some crucial respects different in the financial markets because the nature of the relationship between employer and employee is significantly different. The relationship between trader and employer in the markets has more of the ethos of a contract between two individual parties based on mutual interest than of a conventional employer/employee relationship. Traders tend to see themselves as practitioners of a craft more than as long-term employees of the institution. And many traders are footloose: relatively few spend the whole of their working careers with one employer. In fact, it is not uncommon for individual career histories to show four or five different employers over a dozen years. In the world of the financial markets, the labour market is as fluid and competitive as anything else. Everything has its price – including trading experience.

This sense of self-employment derives from knowing what they are good at. Traders with experience and a track record have a strong belief in their own abilities. Moreover, they are perpetually excited about the markets; as acting is to an actor, trading is in their bloodstream. Movement in the markets is like manna from heaven; seeing movement and believing that you know what will happen next is to be alive. To pick exactly the right moment to take a profit – selling out from a position in dollars, in bonds or in shares just as the market reaches a peak – is ecstasy. The clenched fist and the yelp of triumph are the same as when a crucial ace is served during a tense Wimbledon final: *you won*. The psychological upsurge from beating the market is every bit as powerful as the thrill of winning at poker or in a closely fought game of tennis.

And like the successful tennis pro – or the successful Hollywood star – good traders can expect generous pay. To the rest of the world, perhaps, their life seems like a hell of stress and bedlam. Ironically, though, many are doing what they most enjoy – *and* are compensated (to use the elegant term favoured throughout the commercial world these days) handsomely for it. The rewards are high indeed for those who are good. In the markets, bonuses tied closely to profit performance are a major component of take-home pay. But there is another side of the coin too. There is little security, and the threat of being fired (or 'terminated', to use the slightly sinister-sounding term now in widespread use) for poor perfor-mance is ever-present. This is a business with little room for passengers, and all of those involved know that.

As a result, there is little or no hypocrisy about the nature of the employment relationship or of the rewards. As we have seen, unremitting competition is the motor of the markets. The institutions have to be at their best or they risk elimination, and none can rest on their laurels for long. The house that misses its footing loses its best people, poached by competitors. Poor profit performance can lead rapidly to lay-offs as firms struggle to reduce costs, which are dominated by the costs of the people they employ. In this environment it is hardly surprising that traders seek to control their own destiny. They neither want nor expect cradle-to-grave employment. They are not prepared to wait for the gold watch and the retirement pension. The aim is financial independence – and as soon as possible.

All of which underlines the impression that life in the City is different. There is a huge gulf between the career expectations of a dealer and of the banker the public meets in a high-street branch – or, indeed, of a nurse, teacher or car-assembly worker. Few dealers expect to be working up to a normal retirement age. Ask dealers in their thirties what they hope to be doing when they are fifty, and virtually none will answer that they expect to be in a dealing room. Ambition often focuses on what to do after an early retirement from active service in the markets. There are plenty of actual cases of traders quitting the markets to do such things as running a pizza parlour or small restaurant in the country, or a vineyard in Provence. Asked about their intentions, traders will give answers as varied as their individual personalities: one will look forward to a life of leisure, rotating between the Cotswolds and a Caribbean island; another may want to study for a degree; a third may talk of working with disadvantaged children. Others have wandered far and wide. Jim Rogers, an American investment manager, decided at the age of thirty-seven to quit his highly paid job in Wall Street and took off with his girlfriend to ride round the world on a motorbike. He wrote a best-selling book about the experience, mixing travelogue with sharp analysis of economic and investment possibilities wherever he went. He concluded that

> ... if you' ve got a dream, you have to try it;
> you must get it out of your system. You will
> never get another chance.[3]

This is hardly a new thought, but market people are perhaps more likely than many others to put it into practice because they are natural initiators – and because they have more money.

None of this means, however, that those who work in the markets have no interest in the performance of their employing institution. They have, in fact, a very clear interest, since their 'compensation' is typically tied in part to the profit performance of the institution. But there is generally also another, deeper level of interest. Individualists though they often seem to be, market people nevertheless identify psychologically with the competitive success of their firms. To be high in the rankings – to have the largest share of the foreign exchange market, or to be the biggest bond underwriter, or to have the best stock research analysts – these are the kinds of goals which City firms aspire to, and their traders easily identify with them.

This competitive team instinct is not, of course, unique to the City; it is a feature of any commercial activity. From the point of view of market efficiency, it makes no difference what the deeply buried origins of the competitive instinct are. So long as traders do compete – and so long as no institution ever wins[4] – the markets will do what they are supposed to do: they will serve as efficient mechanisms for balancing supply and demand at the best price.

But the question is, what does all this do to the players? What is the *spiritual* effect of all the pressure to perform, and of the naked reward system? As far as the institutions which compete in the markets are concerned, they are apt to behave as if the competition were a matter of life and death – as if, in fact, they were engaged in a war. Indeed, the language of competition often sounds like preparation for war. Business tactics are discussed in terms borrowed from military strategy: the aim is to outflank the competitors, capture the high ground, mount dawn raids, and so on.

For the individual, however, there *has* to be a balance. The individual, after all, is a being with eternal significance in the sight of God; the institution is not. When a venerable firm with a long pedigree collapses or is taken over, we may shed a tear for the passing of a famous old name. But it is the human beings involved – not the institutions – that are ultimately precious. And human beings cannot – or rather, should not – treat their careers as a matter of life and death. The whole thrust of this book is that the markets have a valuable role in human affairs, from which it follows that the competition which is the essence of the markets has its legitimacy. But although we compete freely in the markets, we do so – or should do so – without attributing life-and-death significance to the results. For individuals, commercial life should not become the psychological equivalent of war.

To put the point differently, the best way of keeping a healthy approach to commercial competition is to treat it as a *game*. Not in the sense of being trivial and worth only casual effort, but as a game to be played with dedication, skill and in pursuit of excellence – a game in which both those who win and those who do not can be said to have contributed to an excellent overall result. The real comparison, in other words, should be with, say, a game of rugby or perhaps with an athletics tournament (an analogy which may fit the individualism of traders better) – not with the art of war. Those who lose this perspective, and begin psychologically to treat competition in the markets as more of a war than a game, succumb almost inevitably to the great occupational hazard of commercial life – it becomes the ultimate end of their existence.

Those who lose perspective can all too easily become obsessively addicted to winning at any cost. And the addiction may even extend to winning against the rules. This is the route travelled by Gekko. Unfortunately,

Gekko is not alone: he has enough real life followers who are prepared to be drawn into the shadowy world of fraud and insider dealing in pursuit of the big prize. But at least there is a clear line between breaking the law and not doing so. Some are prepared to cross this line, but the vast majority are not. There is even a fairly clear distinction between sailing close to the wind and genuine integrity – a distinction which any who are honest with themselves recognize. More, perhaps, are prepared to cross this line, but again, most are not.

Yet even for those who take pride in their business integrity, and who would never dream of indulging in the insider dealing of which Gekko is past master, there remains the subtle danger of being lured by the prospect of *power* into giving too much of themselves to their career. The evidence is that, time and time again, people run the risk of workaholism – of sacrificing leisure interests, social lives, friendships and even family life to their god of success. The stories are all too common. One executive, after doing well in his career, takes off a sabbatical six months – notionally in order to do some post-graduate study but in practice to have more time with his family. He returns to work confessing how much this time has made him realize what he missed because he was away so much when his children (now in their late teens) were small. Or a trader known for a brilliant mind and decisive trading style, and regarded as having great potential, is suddenly shaken by losses as the market unexpectedly moves against all his positions. Hunched over his desk, with grey rings round his eyes, he struggles to cover his losses. Suddenly he explodes in rage at the poor quality of the screen information, lashes out at the management whose fault it all is – both the incompetent computer and the fickle market – and quits, quits the City completely, leaving a promising career behind him. Or the investment manager who has built up a successful business over the years only to find himself involved in an acrimonious divorce which is ruinously expensive and drains all his enthusiasm. There is nothing left, for he knows of nothing else to be enthusiastic about.

Unfortunately, such cautionary tales are not only of those who have discovered before reaching their goal what it is to give too much. Those who do get to the top of whatever peak they have set themselves to climb have been known to find that the glory melts like snow in their hand. Sooner or later they notice some other, higher peak they cannot reach. Sooner or later they notice that the peak they are on is lonely. Maybe there are some who are not only successful in satisfying their driving ambition but also happy and at peace with the world and with themselves. But perhaps not many? 'The want of a thing is perplexing enough, but the possession of it is intolerable.'[5] So said an early eighteenth-century wit, who might have been speaking for some, at least, of today's most successful market players and financial magnates.

If power and success are subtly seductive, then there is something else which is even more pervasive, and certainly more blatant: the pull of materialism. Greed is widespread. For many in the markets, money – and what it can buy – is the great prize. Greed for money is not the same as the seduction of power. It is in a sense more democratic, and perhaps less insidious. Power is exclusive; it cannot be shared or it is not power. By contrast, others can have money without it necessarily detracting from your own. Greed is not the same as envy. On the whole, envy is the weapon used by mammon to enslave those who do not have access to wealth, whereas greed is the way it enslaves those who do. So greed (more than envy) is the besetting sin of the markets.

In any event, whether it is greed or envy makes no real difference: money has a powerful hold. Even if the pull of money is different from the pull of power, it can become a demanding god for those who work in the markets, just as surely as power can. The rewards are high enough – which in theory should mean that traders have the advantage of reaching the point where basic needs are taken care of much faster, and thus should open up all kinds of opportunities (as we shall see in Chapter 7). In practice, however, there is something notoriously elastic about the concept of a basic need. The loss of perspective can be breathtaking. In fact, it is not unknown for those who work in the markets actually to feel *short* of money. In *The Bonfire of the Vanities* Sherman McCoy constantly laments the way in which his money 'haemorrhages away' as he struggles to keep up with his family's extravagant lifestyle on an income of around $1 million.

* * *

We are all servants of something. The only question is, what? Jesus called his followers to be servants in the kingdom of God and taught that this kingdom has absolute priority. He allows us – indeed, he encourages us – to stay at work in the world, but on the basis that we do what we do because it advances that kingdom. If we serve God first, and love our neighbour as ourselves, we will find rewards that have real spiritual value. But there is no middle ground. The evidence of human experience is that other gods will fill a spiritual vacuum. When we serve other gods sooner or later we realize that we have become slaves. We find ourselves cheated – because ambition goes unachieved; because family life has collapsed around us; because sickness reminds us of mortality; or even just because we find ourselves waking up in the middle of the night, glaringly conscious that there must be something more to our lives than the power and the glory and the wealth. The rude awakening may not come for years, but one way or another it does come.

Encounters with Jesus were often the cause of such rude awakenings. There is one encounter in particular – recorded in more or less the same way in Matthew, Mark and Luke – which could have taken place yesterday on the steps of the Royal Exchange in the City of London or at the Stock Exchange in Wall Street, so pointed and disturbing are its implications for those who work in commerce and the financial world. This is the encounter with a young man who is known simply for the fact that he was rich.

What is interesting about this man is that he was by all accounts a person of integrity. This was no Gordon Gekko. We are not told whether the wealth came from family inheritance or from judicious business dealing: it does not matter. This rich young man stands for all those who work in environments like the City and have prospered. The point of the story is sharpened by the fact that he is an honourable man of strong moral principles. In this encounter Jesus is not out to make points about honesty;

the requirement for strict honesty in all commercial dealings is simply assumed by both parties. The point is something much more profound.

We know this from the very first question: 'What
must I do to inherit eternal life?' Why is someone as well
endowed as he was, with all that a successful commercial
life can bring, even asking this question? Because one of
the oldest lessons in the book is that wealth does not
satisfy. Down the ages, humans have learnt this truth and
expressed it in many different cultures. The Greek story of
Midas is but one example. Midas considers himself unbe-
lievably fortunate to have been given the gift of turning
anything he touches into gold – until he gradually finds
himself cut off from all human contact and left alone in his
palace of cold gold. So no, wealth is not enough. What
must I do to inherit eternal life?

On the face of it, the answer is simple and known to
both parties: keep God's laws. The young man had done so
– on the surface. The Ten Commandments would have been
his watchword. We can presume that he was a man who
took his family responsibilities seriously. He would have
also been scrupulous in keeping the Sabbath. As far as
his personal and commercial behaviour was concerned, his
conduct was presumably exemplary. Jesus summarizes the
Ten Commandments for him and he responds: 'Teacher, I
have kept all these from my youth.' In which case, what is
the point of the conversation?

However, in any such encounter, when we intend to
bare our anguish, it is all too easy to be only half honest.
And so it was. The Great Counsellor knew this:

> Jesus, looking at him, **loved him** and said,
> ' You lack one thing; go, sell what you own,
> and give the money to the poor, and you
> will have treasure in heaven; then come,
> follow me.' (Mark 10:21)

The phrase in bold type is in Mark's account, although not in the accounts of Matthew and Luke. It is an invaluable touch, which reminds us of the source of Jesus' power in such encounters. The Counsellor counselled in love. That love was the source of the crucial insight about the young man: *his integrity was not enough.*

The truth was that he was possessed by his wealth. No doubt he thought that *he* possessed his wealth, but *it* possessed him. What he had in effect done was to break one of those Ten Commandments he was so proud of having kept from his youth, and he had paid the price. Though he may have been a man of integrity, and taken his social and family responsibilities seriously, he had ended up – perhaps only gradually and apparently without being fully aware of the fact – idolizing his wealth. In so doing he was breaking one of the Commandments:

> You shall not make for yourself an idol,
> whether in the form of anything that is in
> heaven above, or that is on the earth
> beneath, or that is in the water under the
> earth. You shall not bow down to them or
> worship them ... (Exodus 20: 4 – 5a)

Not that the young man had done this in any literal sense.

That was the last thing a self respecting religious man of his background and his day would have done. But just as clearly he had done it in a spiritual sense.

There are many people who do so today. Though their whole thought world is miles apart from that of the rich and religious young man of Jesus' time, they too might be surprised to be told that they were breaking a commandment about worshipping idols (even if they would freely concede breaking a number of the other Commandments!). But the fact is that, just as surely as he was, there are many who work in the markets as slaves to the gods of wealth and power.

Jesus' response is tailored to the person. What has become an addiction has to be broken. Gentle measures are not enough. It is no use telling alcoholics to cut down on their drinking. They have to give it up, totally. Former alcoholics will say, even many years later, that it would take only one drink to bring them down again. Indeed, former alcoholics will often say that there is no such thing as a former alcoholic: alcoholic is what they are, and alcohol remains off-limits for the rest of their lives. Though it is a thought that shocks, Jesus treats this man and his obsession with wealth as if he were an alcoholic. Break your addiction now, and do it the only way you can. You will find a whole new enrichment from the total reorientation of your life that will then become possible. Liquidate all your assets and give the proceeds to the poor. Follow a new master – and then you will have treasure in heaven.

How does the young man respond to the challenge? Unfortunately, by ducking it. As the poignantly understated account puts it:

When he heard this, he was shocked and went away grieving, for he had many possessions. (Mark 10:22)

The whole of the man's spiritual dilemma is encapsulated in those last few words – and it shows the seriousness of the matter. This encounter does not have a happy ending. We know from the uncomfortably close parallel of physical addictions that this can all too often be true. Alcoholics do not always break the addiction; drug use can be terrible to shake off; so too can spiritual addictions such as the rich young man's obsession with wealth. When such spiritual addictions do not have physical effects, or when the addict ignores that all-important first step of recognizing the addiction for what it is, it can be even harder than it sometimes is for alcoholics.

It would be wrong, however, to treat Jesus' words to this man as being a general prescription for all those who are well paid and working in the commercial and financial world. There is no doubt that his *ad hominem* call to give up all and follow him into a new life should certainly be heard by many, who would be released and enriched beyond their deepest yearnings if they took this call to heart. But it is not Jesus' general guidance. As we have seen, he does not tell Zacchaeus the tax collector, for example, to leave his occupation, nor does he tell him to give up all his wealth. Jesus associated freely with the rich as well as the poor of his day. He dined happily with affluent establishment figures, even if they often found him disturbing. Certainly, he constantly warns of the great spiritual risks of riches. But his main purpose was to liberate people for the service of God. Whether or not that requires the sacrifice of a person's wealth depends on the particular person and the spiritual circumstances. It does not for Zacchaeus; it does for the rich young man.

In fact, Jesus' general guidance on wealth and power is contained not in his dealings with the rich young man, but in teaching which is included by Matthew in what is commonly known as the Sermon on the Mount:

> No one can serve two masters; for a servant will either hate the one and love the other, or be devoted to the one and despise the other. You cannot serve God and Mammon.
>
> Therefore I tell you, do not worry about your life, what you will eat or what you will drink; or about your body, what you will wear. Is not life more than food, and the body more than clothing? Look at the birds of the air; they neither sow nor reap nor gather into barns; and yet your heavenly Father feeds them. Are you not of more value than they? And can any of you by worrying add a single hour to your span of life? And why do you worry about clothing? Consider the lilies of the field, how they grow; they neither toil nor spin, yet I tell you, even Solomon in all his glory was not clothed like one of these. But if God so clothes the grass of the field, which is alive today and tomorrow is thrown into the

oven, will he not much more clothe you –
you of little faith? Therefore do not worry,
saying, ' What will we eat?' or ' What will
we drink?' or ' What will we wear?' ... But
strive first for the kingdom of God and his
righteousness, and all these things will be
given to you as well. (Matthew 6:24 – 33) [6]

It is clear what this amounts to: a call to sit lightly with wealth and all it brings. A pedantic rationalist might pick it apart for what might be seen as an overly romantic and idealized view of life. (After all, the sceptic might say, the birds of the air are in fact engaged in an unremitting struggle for survival.) But that is to miss the point – which is a simple one, expressed in unforgettable imagery: do not become the slave of mammon. Wealth and power carry real risks. If you have them, remember why they are given to you, and what your priorities are. Remember how unimportant to your true self and its real satisfaction they are. If your priorities are right, you will sit loose with them. You will use them – or lose them – as the call of God demands.

Many would be tempted to question whether this can ever be anything more than a pious hope. The pressures and the incentives of an abrasive work environment and a materialistic society surely make it inevitable that the individual will succumb. How can it be possible to give ten or twelve hours a day to such an energy sapping environment and still be able, genuinely, to sit lightly with all its blandishments?

The inescapable fact, however, is that Jesus never did offer easy options. Whether his call was to stay in the world of business (Zacchaeus) or to shake it off (the rich young man), it was a call for radical change. Those who think his teaching on how to deal with the risks of wealth and power is easy to follow are of course fooling themselves. Yet Jesus does indeed claim that it is the only possible way, and still he does call some to take the risk of being there in the world of business and finance. His disciples who are with him at the encounter with the rich young man are rightly amazed at the difficulty of it all. Jesus reminds them that for human beings in their own strength it is effectively impossible – but not for God. For God, all things are possible (see Mark 10: 23 – 27). Without that conviction, the call to sit lightly with material things and to ignore the siren voices of wealth and power would indeed be nothing but a pious hope.

NOTES

1 It may be that this reflects the lingering British fastidiousness about the world of money and trade. Americans have never had the same reluctance to recognize its existence. Their literary talent has therefore been more ready to see it as a source of material.

2 See Michael Lewis, *Liar's Poker* (New York: W.W. Norton, 1989).

3 See Jim Rogers, *Investment Biker* (New York: Random House, 1994).

4 If any institution ever gained monopoly power in the markets, their workings would be seriously distorted. However, whilst the risk of monopoly exists in some markets, there is no real reason to fear this possibility in the major global financial markets – which are highly competitive and where barriers to entry by new competitors are low.

5 Sir John Vanbrugh, *The Confederacy*, I.iii.46 – 47.

6 It is worth noting that Luke's Gospel puts the main part of this teaching at a different point – not in the group of sayings known as the Sermon on the Mount, but later on. He puts it directly after a parable about a man who stores up more and more produce in bigger and bigger barns, only to hear God say to him, 'You fool! This very night your life is being demanded of you ...' So it is, the parable concludes acerbically, with those who store up treasures for themselves but are not rich toward God.

6

Christians in the Markets: Called to Take Risk

Legend has it that the medieval scholar and conjuror Dr Faustus sold his soul to the devil in return for twenty-four years during which the devil would be his servant and fulfil his every desire. For twenty-four years he accumulates wealth, indulges his fantasies and shamelessly enjoys himself. In the last half-hour, as the clock ticks remorselessly towards midnight, he bitterly regrets the bargain he has struck and grasps desperately for salvation. But there is no escape. As midnight chimes, the devil claims his own ...

Is that what those who work in the markets are doing? Do we sell our souls for all the excitement and the lure of money? In past centuries, the answer of the Christian Church was, in effect, yes. And that old feeling that the world of finance is somehow beyond the pale still occasionally surfaces in pronouncements from Christian sources. According to some, the City still sups with the devil. But we have to proclaim that this is wrong. In the eighteenth and nineteenth centuries, Christian thinking found it difficult enough to come to terms with the Industrial Revolution and its apparently debasing effect on the human spirit. In his famous poem 'Jerusalem' William Blake asks

> *And was Jerusalem builded here*
> *Among these dark satanic mills?*

Blake had his own mysterious answer to that question, but for thousands of ordinary Christians the 'dark satanic mills' conjured up a vision of grimy labyrinths beyond the reach of the Spirit of God. In a strange sense, the City and the financial markets have been the twentieth-century equivalent of those dark Satanic mills for the Church – a world which is not at all dark and grimy in any visual sense, but which is still a no-go area for the Spirit of God.

But it is clear that the Spirit of God is indeed there. And Christians should be there. Life in the markets is ambiguous, certainly, but so is life in other fields. The markets are not perfect, but nor is any other human activity. Trading depends on an instinct for competitive gain, but that is true of all human commerce. The competitive instinct can become obsessive and unbalanced, for sure. But it is not intrinsically wrong, any more than the desire to excel in, say, athletic competition is wrong. It needs to be fettered by law and regulation where appropriate; and it needs to be developed within a shared moral framework which places public value on integrity in commercial practice and on care for the weak. Where these conditions prevail, the competitive instinct is fully compatible with the basic commandment to love our neighbours as ourselves.

The overwhelming evidence points to the importance of effectively functioning markets in fostering economic development. Sometimes, writers – including Christian writers – from the 'new right' of the 1980s have been too complacent about the benefits of free markets and unwilling to pay enough attention to the policy measures – both national and international – needed to ensure that markets are not distorted in their operation. But the fact remains that it has proven impossible to find any substitute which works nearly as well and which does not compromise human freedom to a dangerous degree.

That being the case, we should *expect* to find the kingdom of God in the midst of the markets. There are, of course, risks: opportunities for wealth and power are more freely available in the markets than in many other fields of human endeavour. Correspondingly, the risks of seduction are greater. People do give too much of themselves to the competition; people do become possessed by wealth and power. But the risk of seduction for one reason or another is everywhere: not just in the thick of the markets, but in small rural communities, in the halls of academia and in cathedral precincts. Some might think that the only way of avoiding contamination is to opt out and become a hermit or join some contemplative community, but even that course is not free from spiritual hazards. In any case, most of us have no inclination to do any such thing. Christ sends his followers into – not out of – the world, even though he clearly acknowledges its dangers. In fact, he not only tells his followers to stay in the midst of the world, he counsels them not to be naïve in their dealings in it:

> *See, I am sending you out like sheep into*
> *the midst of wolves:*
> *so be wise as serpents and harmless as*
> *doves.* (Matthew 10:16)

As advice for involvement in the markets, this could hardly be more direct and to the point. It is a striking series of images which recognizes that there is risk involved. In the context of the markets, the wolves become a metaphor for the dangers of money and power. The Christian in that world needs a wisdom which can almost be described as 'street-wise' and based on all the earthy common sense associated with the image of the serpent. Yet the Christian is also called to be as gentle as a dove (with its associations of peace), without any of the deceitful cunning of the serpent.

The first and most basic question, therefore, as far as the individual Christian who works – or is contemplating working – in the markets in any capacity is concerned is: are you *called* to be there? We have seen that the traditional Christian view of what constituted a calling from God was very narrow. Up until medieval times, having a vocation meant that you were called out of the secular world into a religious vocation. From about the sixteenth century onwards it gradually became acceptable to talk of being called into secular activities. But in practice, as reflected in everyday usage, the idea of vocation was restricted to careers whose purpose could not be measured in terms of profit. Thus teachers, doctors and nurses might all have vocations – but not a merchant banker (or an industrialist). Indeed, when I graduated from university in 1969 (in those halcyon days when graduate unemployment was virtually unknown, and when the only difficulty graduates faced in the job market was in deciding which career alternative to pursue), my fellow students were heading off in all sorts of different directions. One was a medical student who was working towards becoming a medical missionary in Africa. She – we all understood – had a very clear calling. Another wanted to teach in Liverpool: he certainly felt he had a calling to this. Yet another was on course to become a solicitor in Dorset: we might even have recognized that he had a calling to serve the community. But the idea that joining a merchant bank could be considered the outcome of God's calling would have seemed strange, even faintly hypocritical. After all, it was clear that you did that for the money, not in order to serve humanity.

Implicit in this way of thinking and use of language was an acceptance that those following a vocation were paid less than those in commerce and finance. The vocation was its own reward. Conversely, people in commerce, industry and finance were part of a world which was treated as though it consisted essentially of work which was unpleasant and spiritually unrewarding; a world in which people worked because they needed the money and would not be doing it if they did not have to. In this world, hours worked were hours taken away from the real purpose of life; they were a means to an end, which was fulfilled not in the workplace but outside it. When City jargon describes pay as 'compensation' it is tapping into this deeply rooted understanding of the nature of work.

It is clear, however, that Christians in the financial world ought not to accept this view of their work life. For one thing, the cynic might say that the truth is in many cases almost the exact opposite: those who work in the markets have an uproarious time – the last thing they need is to think of their considerable pay as being compensation. In any case, if the markets contribute to human development, then it is not sufficient to regard the hours worked there as being undertaken simply as a means to other ends. The individual's contribution may be only a tiny component of the whole. If you work, for example, on developing management information systems for one part of the business of one bank in one sector of the markets, the connection between what you do and the progress of human development as a whole may seem remote. But that does not mean that the connection does not exist. Nor does it alter its value to the kingdom of God, which is a city built of innumerable bricks, most of which look infinitesimal in relation to the whole. In other words, if the work can be identified as contributing, in however small a way, to the kingdom of God, then it warrants our full Christian commitment.

George Herbert, the great English Christian poet of the early seventeenth century, wrote of this commitment to work in his famous hymn:

> *Teach me, my God and King,*
> *in all things thee to see;*
> *and what I do in anything*
> *to do it as for thee ...*
>
> *All may of thee partake;*
> *nothing can be so mean*
> *which, with this tincture, 'For thy sake',*
> *will not grow bright and clean ...*

This is the famous stone
that turneth all to gold;
for that which God doth touch and own
cannot for less be told.

Through the slightly archaic English of this poem from over three and a half centuries ago resonates an understanding of the value of work in God's kingdom which is as important for us today as when it was written. Nothing can be so mean: no contribution is too insignificant for the kingdom. If the work is done 'for thy sake' – with all that this implies – it will have its effect and will be precious in God's sight. This is the famous stone: that is, the touchstone which medieval philosophers believed would turn everything into gold. They never found such a stone, of course, but work for God's kingdom is worth all the gold there is. The work, therefore, should have its own compensation. If it does not, then a Christian should not be doing it. (We will come back to the question of the implications of all this for a Christian understanding of what the world calls compensation – i.e. pay – shortly.)

Yet the Christian understanding of work as vocation requires even more than that. It is not enough to satisfy ourselves that our work contributes to the kingdom of God. We are required also to be sure that *we personally* are called to that particular work, for that is the implication of the New Testament commission to the followers of Christ. In the extraordinarily rich language of John's Gospel, the Christian's commission is an extension of Christ's own ministry. Jesus prays to the Father on behalf of his followers:

*As you have sent me into the world, so I have
sent them into the world ... I ask not only on
behalf of these, but also on behalf of those
who will believe in me through their word,
that they may all be one ...* (John 17:18–21a)

It would be easy to miss the relevance of this to the world of work. Christians are called to see themselves as sent into the world, collectively commissioned to do Christ's work. The commission concerns us all, and affects all parts of our lives. That includes our work lives.

Churches of virtually all denominations have to a greater or lesser extent diluted the impact of this commission by accepting a division of their members into two groups: those who are in full-time Christian ministry and leadership, and those who are not – who as a result play a largely passive role. The consequence has been the loss of that vibrant sense that *all* Christians are sent into the world as Christ's ministers. We have to recover that commitment. We have to remember, for example, that Paul simply assumed that *all* Christians were following a calling that embraced the whole of their lives. He writes to the querulous Corinthians in terms which remind them that, in the eyes of what might be considered the religious or cultural establishment of their day, they have no credentials – and yet they are called (see Corinthians 1:26). And the letter to the Colossians exhorts them

*... whatever you do, in word or deed, do
everything in the name of the Lord Jesus ...*
(Colossians 3:17)

The principle is unambiguous: it is an insistent theme of the New Testament that *all* Christians are called to serve, and that this calling embraces *all* parts of our lives. Despite the obvious differences between the circumstances and expectations of those early Christians and ourselves, it is clear what we should have in common: an understanding that whatever we do with our lives must be shaped by the over-arching fact of our calling. Calling – vocation – is not limited to special roles in Christian ministry, nor is it restricted to certain professional roles which do not appear to be sullied by the profit motive.[1] God calls each of us to work for his kingdom. And God calls some Christians to work in the financial markets.

The implications of this for us as individuals are profoundly challenging. Too many of us – Christians as well as others – drift through our work lives without any sense of whether we are called to be doing what we do. We start a particular career because we like what we understand of the work involved, or because it is expected of us, or just because that was the door that happened to open. In the case of the financial markets, many are attracted by the excitement and by the prospect of high rewards; few would claim any sort of vocation.

But as time goes by, we often become entrenched in our careers and find our identity increasingly changed by them. For some, the career which started out with high hopes remains stretching and exciting – and becomes an ever more important part of our lives. For others, their career experience is less rewarding: it does not stimulate (either because it never did from the first, or because promotion does not come, or because familiarity breeds boredom). There is plenty of white-collar drudgery in financial world: there are many for whom Monday is systematically the worst day of the week and Friday the best; people for whom their work is just a job, not a career; people who long for retirement, even if they have no realistic idea of what to do with it. I once knew an executive who had a chart on his office wall which was divided into boxes, one for each week of the five years to his retirement. As each week went by, he put a cross through one more box. But even in these circumstances we find ourselves moulded by our job. Even if we are not fully stretched or satisfied by it, even if we feel uncreative or undervalued, our career affects our whole outlook. Our self-esteem – for good or ill – is bound up with it. We become what we do. How often do we find, for example, that the small-talk amongst strangers at a cocktail party focuses almost immediately on what a person does (or worse, what the person's spouse does) at work? We are defined by what we do.

Indeed, this is such a dominant impulse that most of us, whether Christians or not, internalize it. As Christians we are all too often more willing to acknowledge our career than our faith. Because it is socially acceptable to do so, we allow ourselves to be defined by our work, but are often coy about being labelled by our faith. What is my profession? The socially acceptable answer is that I am a banker. But what is my profession? That is, what do I profess? My profession *is* – or should be – that the Way of Jesus Christ is the way of redemption and fulfilment. And my work is – or should be – the particular way I am called to live out that profession.

Why is that such an alien thought? Why do we often find it so difficult to see our career in the framework of faith? Although few of us have any sense of being called into our work lives, yet we typically spend more of our waking hours in that life than in any other activity. In the markets, as we have noted, ten- or even twelve-hour days are commonplace. That amounts to over half the waking lives of those involved, and a much higher proportion of their reserves of energy and creativity. We only have one life to live – only one endowment of gifts and creativity, only the one opportunity to serve in God's kingdom. If we have neither the conviction that what we do is advancing the kingdom, nor the sense that we personally are called to be doing it, then we have not faced this challenge squarely.

Yet Christians need to make the all-important shift. If they want to take the New Testament commission seriously, they cannot afford to drift into and through any career, and certainly not through a career in an environment as demanding as the financial markets. In a sense, the choice is stark: either they are following God's call when they work in the markets, or they run the grave risk of being reshaped by them, to the point where they sleep, eat and breathe them day after day. They run the risk, in short, of being defined by their job rather than by the call to follow Christ.

So the first step is simple (simple to state, that is – but immensely difficult to implement in reality). Christians in the market-place are called to see themselves as there, not by chance or through drift or because it is the way to wealth or to excitement, but because God wants them, personally, to work in that corner of his kingdom.

And how does a Christian discover that calling? The

same way, essentially, as we discover anything else about God's purposes for us. Prayer must play a central role, and the counsel of other Christians plays a supporting role. In that process of prayer and counsel we need to have our motives put to the test. Why do you think this is the right thing to do? Are you looking to the financial rewards to build up the capacity for Christian service and giving? Or are you really turned on by what the money can buy? Or even just by the thought of being wealthy as an end in itself? Do you believe in the value of the work? Or are you just enthused by the excitement of it all? We all discover in our journeys through life as Christians just how easy it can be to deceive ourselves as to our real motives – to delude ourselves that some course of action is the will of God, when it is in fact only the will of ourselves. So we need to look to prayer and Christian counsel to put the spotlight on our sense of calling. Is this the Spirit moving in our lives – or not?

For the rest, it involves applying Jesus' guidance to his followers: to be wise as serpents. In other words, apply all the tests of realistic common sense: Is the job interesting? Is it doable? Do you trust your employers? Do they have a coherent and viable business strategy? Do they promote a culture of fairness and meritocracy in the institution? And so on.

What, then, about those who are in the midst of their careers – perhaps carrying family and other responsibilities which make it difficult to contemplate any radical alternatives – and yet deeply dissatisfied and increasingly convinced that they are *not* where they are called to be? There are certainly many Christians who would acknowledge being in this position. What are they supposed to do about their work lives? To people in such circumstances, all this talk of calling can easily seem nothing but pious emptiness.

Clearly, there are no standard remedies, no slick answers which are adequate to all such circumstances. All that can be said in general about the dilemma of those who gain no spiritual satisfaction out of their work lives is that Christians in such situations should hold on to the conviction that God does not intend them simply to resign themselves to their fate. Though the way out of the spiritual dilemma may be far from clear, it is surely right to confront the issue and recognize it for what it is, rather than bury it and just soldier on.

The answer is, in fact, the same as for the young person trying to discover a calling for the first time: prayer and Christian counsel, but without any pretence that it is easy. In the end, the answer may be a new discovery that there is work of God's to do within that work sphere which has seemed so dry and unsatisfying. Or there may be no alternative to accepting the work sphere for what it is, in which case the answer may be to seek some other avenue of activity (at weekends or in evenings) which offers Christian fulfilment. Or a door may open into something else altogether. The only certainty is that God calls us; we have to find the power to listen.

NOTES

1 Nor is a calling to be equated, as has happened in the past, with the class system. The concept of a divinely ordered social structure

in which each was called to a particular station is reflected in a verse – now generally omitted – from the highly popular Victorian hymn 'All things bright and beautiful' which went:

> The rich man in his castle,
> The poor man at his gate;
> God made them high or lowly
> And ordered their estate.

Fortunately, we are now beyond this static and unliberated view of society and of Christian calling. We can – and must – recapture the dynamism and comprehensiveness of the original Christian view of individual calling.

7

Christians in the Markets: Accepting Responsibility

With God's calling – to the markets or any other vocation – goes the challenge to accept responsibility. One of the stories Jesus told concerns three servants, each of whom is entrusted with a sum of money by their employer, who is leaving for a long journey. The sums involved are large. One is given five talents (a Greek coin of great value), one is given two talents, and the third is given one talent. In our currency, say, £5,000, £2,000 and £1,000 respectively (or maybe we should multiply those numbers by 100) – the specific amounts do not matter. The story is not about investment management, it is about all that we have to contribute to the kingdom of God – our abilities, aptitudes and energy, as well as our time and money:

> *For the kingdom of heaven is as if a man,*
> *going on a journey, summoned his servants*
> *and entrusted his property to them; to one*
> *he gave five talents, to another two, to*

another one, to each according to his
ability. Then he went away. The one who
had received the five talents went off at
once and traded with them, and made five
more talents. In the same way, the one who
had the two talents made two more talents.
But the one who had received the one
talent went off and dug a hole in the
ground, and hid his master's money ...
(Matthew 25:14–29)

This story reminds us of two crucial points about Christians in their work life. First, we *all* have capabilities in different measures. One servant was given five talents, one was given two, the third was given one; no one was given none. In reality, some seem to have had abilities and blessings showered on them: they are bright, extrovert, attractive, energetic and enjoy good health. They have money and opportunities, and the world seems to be their oyster. They are people who seem naturally to become the centre of attention and do well in whatever they turn their hands to. There are others who sense that they have little to offer and that they spend their lives on the periphery of things. Some are natural leaders; others feel as though no one would notice if they were not there. But Jesus' story tells us that all of us have a contribution to make to God's kingdom. All of us have talents (to use the word in its everyday sense, not to refer to a Greek coin), all of us have resources; and God calls all of us to use them. The third servant's failure was not that he had only modest resources, but that he did not use what he had. He went for the risk-free option which involved no commitment, and for this he is condemned by his master on his return.

Secondly, what we are given is, in one important sense, not a gift. This story reminds us that God gives us resources not as free gifts to do what we like with. Not even the third servant – who simply buries his talent, rather than making profit from it for the master – feels free to go off and spend his cash on a new car or a Caribbean holiday. God gives us resources to use *in his service*, in the advancement of his kingdom. These gifts confer responsibility. If we do not put our talents, our energy, our resources to use – or if we use them simply to further our own ends – then the consequences are grave in God's sight, even if we ourselves are hardly aware of the scale of the opportunity lost. For it means that the common good which God wants for all his children is damaged by the loss of our contribution.

This story also reminds us, by its whole setting, that the resources we are given are for use in the context of *work*. In the world of work we are called to use our gifts in the service of the Master. Who is my employer? I know who pays me and whose signature is on my employment contract, but as Christians we acknowledge that our real Master is God. We use *his* gifts for *his* service. So if the key principle is that Christians should work in the markets (or, of course, anywhere else) if and only if they have God's calling to do so, then it follows that they must accept the responsibilities which go with that calling. These responsibilities are of two basic kinds: they must follow their calling with complete integrity; and they must accept that they are stewards, and not (in God's sight) owners, of the resources they acquire through their work.

First, then, the requirement of integrity. The Christian has an unyielding obligation to live by the standards of God's law. That much we have in common with the rich young man whom Jesus confronted. We learn from him that integrity is not enough, but it is certainly necessary. What does this mean in practice? In the context of the market-place and the work of financial institutions, it calls perhaps above all for the avoidance of politicking and for honesty in all dealings.

Politicking deserves special mention in the context of a discussion of business integrity in the financial world because it is one of the great hazards of modern corporate life. Institutions vary widely in the extent and nature of their corporate politics, but none is exempt. Some, for example, seem deliberately to foster a culture of internal competition, on the basis that a Darwinian struggle will produce the strongest leaders. At the other end of the scale, some institutions equally deliberately cultivate the culture of the team player, discouraging both the maverick and the jungle fighter, and prizing consensus and group loyalty. But, whatever the corporate culture, politics will not be wholly absent so long as human beings aspire to power and influence. The politics may be blatant or subtle, fostered or suppressed – but never absent.

For the Christian this poses a sometimes uncomfortable dilemma, as there is a widespread perception that to squeeze the most out of our career requires at a minimum good political antennae, and all too often good skills in manoeuvring and manipulation. It may even require the readiness to clamber on the shoulders of others. There are many seductions: there is the temptation to gossip about who is on the fast track and who is not, whose fortunes are on the wane, who are the dark horses, and so on. There is also the desire to bask in the favour of superiors, leading to such hardy perennials as claiming credit for what goes right and shifting the responsibility for what goes wrong. Many are those who put great skill and effort into 'managing up' whilst displaying a quite different persona when 'managing down'. Above all, there is the pervasive desire to build empires – to own territory, to ensure visibility, to increase our own importance.

What should Christians do about this? I once heard Jackie Pullinger, the famous Christian worker amongst street-sleepers and drug addicts in Hong Kong, address a group of Christian business people. She had them transfixed by her story of life in the raw, such was the stark contrast between their experience and hers. When questioned about the role of Christians at work, she argued that they should wherever possible refuse promotion because the more senior you become, the more you get sucked in, the harder it is to resist the politics, and the less time and energy you have available for Christian work.

Understandable though this view is – and there is little doubt that career advancement brings with it more and more responsibility, which often translates into harder and harder work – it is nevertheless wrong as a general prescription (even if it may well apply to the particular situations of some Christians). It presupposes that same old view of work as a regrettable necessity, of no spiritual value in itself, and to be minimized as far as possible. It overlooks the possibility that God may actually be calling us to accept responsibility at work. Carried to its logical conclusion, it would mean that there were no Christians in any positions of responsibility in the commercial and financial world.

But Christians are not generally called to abjure responsibility. For those who work in the world of finance and commerce, one of the most resonant characters from the Gospel records is the centurion whose servant Jesus heals in Capernaum (see Matthew 8:5–13 and Luke 7: 1–10). Beyond the healing itself what is particularly interesting about this episode are the comments the centurion makes about himself. This is a man who is used to something not unlike modern corporate life. He knows what it is to work within a management structure. He is used to giving and taking orders. He understands what authority is. Without doubt, he would know how authority could be used and misused within his own working environment. He would know about the difficult personnel decisions. Though business life is not the military, and the parallel should not be pushed too far, the centurion with his place in a corporate hierarchy is a man for the modern corporate world. And yet it is striking that there is nothing about the story of his encounter with Jesus which suggests any condemnation of his role.

We certainly need to be aware of the risks of becoming embroiled in office politics, but we are not called to turn our backs on career advancement. What we are required to do is avoid the politics – *all* the manoeuvring, the back-biting and the driving ambition which treats others as means rather than ends, means to *our* ends. There is no question but that this can be a hard road to travel, for anyone with any degree of ambition (and few

Christians are immune from the widespread human urge to get on). To stand back from the politics of the work-place and let career advancement take care of itself is one of the most difficult challenges a Christian in commerce and finance is called to face.

Many Christians would admit that this can require a real internal struggle, and that their success in that struggle is only patchy. For many people, there are few more difficult things to cope with in their work experience than to see a colleague (or even a junior) overtake them up the career ladder. The annoyance is redoubled if they are clearly playing the game we have with difficulty abjured. Yet this *is* what we are called to – a calm acceptance that we will work where we are called to be, to the best of our ability, and leave the career advancement implications to the same God who called us there in the first place.

Then there is the question of honesty. By this I mean the obvious things – expense claims, excessive use of the office phone for personal matters, and so on – but also honesty in subtler areas, especially in the way we deal with colleagues. How, for example, does a manager react to a subordinate who is very able and could therefore be seen as a competitive threat to the manager's own position? Do we let our relationship be infected by the fear of promoting or developing such people? Do we fear to lose them (having come to rely on them)? Does this lead us to distort the way we appraise them? On the other side of the coin, how do we cope with the widespread temptation to opt for half-truths – or even outright whitewash – in appraising subordinates who are performing inadequately? Many in managerial positions prefer to be liked rather than give offence, and are uncomfortable with delivering objective feedback on performance. We avoid the unpalatable truth, preferring to kill with kindness. Difficult conversations are often postponed for years by managers hoping to pass the buck to someone else.

Yet this is one of the most critical functions performed by any manager. Anyone who has any subordinates – whether in secretarial, clerical or managerial roles – has the profoundly important duty of appraising their performance and helping them to fill their potential. The best management practice, of course, acknowledges this as important to the success of the whole institution. It is certainly true of all institutions involved in the financial markets that their most important resource is their people. But as Christians we should recognize an even more important obligation – to serve our neighbour in the name of Christ, and to love our neighbour as ourselves. This requires integrity in dealing with our colleagues in all circumstances, and perhaps above all in the context of performance appraisal, assessment of potential and feedback.

This is not to pretend that honesty is easy. There are many contexts in which brutal honesty is just that – brutal. The person who is not making the grade, the person who has probably 'topped out' and yet passionately wants to go further, the person who is blind to behaviour patterns and weaknesses that are as plain as daylight to all around: it may well require a great deal of sensitivity to deliver home truths to such people in a way that builds, even though it may bruise. This should be no surprise, of course. Dealing with human beings requires wisdom and sensitivity in any context – business, church, family, or otherwise.

These challenges permeate any business life, in the financial markets and elsewhere. The Christian calling is to honesty and integrity in approaching them, though without pretending that the answers are easy. It is sometimes noted that there is a remarkable coincidence between the requirements of Christ's law of love and the precepts of good business management. The call to integrity should not be seen as automatically inconsistent with sound business – as the rich young man would have known. Integrity is certainly not enough, but without it, any claim to be following a Christian calling is simply hypocritical.

Yet although integrity and business are not necessarily oil and water, whether in the financial markets or anywhere else, Christians have to recognize that in certain circumstances integrity may indeed carry a high price. Without in any way seeking martyrdom, they have always to be ready for the possibility of sacrifice should for some reason the two become incompatible. Sacrifice is always a *sotto voce* possibility in the Christian life. Not that we should be melodramatic about it, but we have to recognize that as Christians we may be called to sacrifice our career, however successful it is and however much we may be enjoying it. Something may occur which is directly contrary to Christian principles but which we are asked to condone. We protest, but to no avail. Resignation may seem to be the only acceptable course.

It can happen. Institutions and individuals have both literally broken the law and also behaved in ways which are so morally reprehensible as to make it impossible for any Christian to work with them and still claim to be following God's calling. But experience suggests that such situations are rare. Most issues of commercial and financial morality (other than when a clear breach of the law or a flagrant breach of regulations is involved) are grey, rather than black and white. Moreover, neither individuals nor institutions are perfect. If we are only prepared to join the perfect institution, we will never get a job (or find a church to our taste, either). Nor are we perfect ourselves. So we should remember Jesus' wisdom on the subject of judging others: 'Let anyone who is without sin cast the first stone ...' (John 8:7); and 'First take the log out of your own eye, and then you will see clearly to take the speck out of your neighbour's eye' (Matthew 7:5).

For the individual Christian, the wisest course is surely to seek to work for an institution (or with a group) which values a public reputation as a good corporate citizen, and then to use common sense in deciding what the criterion of morality requires in any particular situation. The task is always to seek to resolve conflicts over what is right through persuasion and reconciliation, not to bring them to the boil as an excuse for some dramatic gesture 'on a point of principle'. The likelihood is that we will go through a whole career without ever confronting a situation which requires us to put our career on the line. Nevertheless, we must not ignore the possibility: situations have arisen in the past, and will do so in the future, when it is right for a Christian to quit on principle. But it is clear that this should be a last resort, based on prayer and after careful testing of our motives: how much self-interest is involved? is our own conduct beyond reproach? are we being self-righteous? are we looking for a way out of a career which is a struggle for us anyway? And so on.

So, the first responsibility of Christians at work is to maintain an integrity which is perfectly compatible with sound business practice, but which in some circumstances may be sacrificial in its cost. The second responsibility is that of stewardship. We are called to recognize that the talents and energies we bring to business are not ours to use as we please, but gifts from God to be used for his purposes. We are also called to recognize the same truth about the resources we accumulate through our work (i.e. the money we earn). In Chapter 5 we noted how highly compensated many who work in the markets are. Moreover, many have (and take) the opportunity of an early departure from the markets. These two facts highlight the opportunities a markets career provides for service outside the career context, and therefore the responsibilities of those Christians who are called to work there.

So far as money is concerned, most in the markets have the potential to become rich by the standards of the vast bulk of humanity – some more so than others, and subjectively, they may not always feel rich. But objectively, both in relation to their needs and in relation to others, few are anything but well off. Christians must see this as nothing more than the gift of resources of which they are stewards. We are not called to refuse acceptance of reasonable market compensation. The market works through the interaction of supply and demand, and if a given degree of experience and potential attracts a given level of compensation, so be it. We owe professionalism and integrity – but not charity – to the market. The only question is: what do we do with the resources of which we become stewards in this way? – resources which can be used for good or ill, squandered on self-indulgence or used for God's kingdom.

The question of what Christians should do with their money is a generic one. All Christians, whatever they have, face the challenge of the New Testament call to share, particularly with the poor. The only difference between Christians who work in the markets and those who work in many other spheres is that they may have more of it, but all are challenged. So far as their financial responsibility is concerned, there are differences only of degree, not of kind. As to what they give their church, to the missions, to aid work or to support particular individuals in need – all this can only emerge from Christ's challenge to each one. We all have to remember that Christ is in those who are in want; to remember that chilling parable of the sheep and the goats: 'Whatever you do – or do not do – to the least of these my children, you do – or do not do – to me' (see Matthew 25:31–46).

The fact that those who work in the markets typically have more money than most should, in theory, make it easier for them to give more. Unfortunately, we all know that this is often not true. The reluctance to give up spending power and financial security seems to endure even when wealth increases. Christ's challenge to support the needy should be easier to meet, the better off we are, but experience tells us that this relationship is a weak one. Yet, whether easy or hard, whether we feel well endowed or not, the challenge remains the same. Much is expected of those to whom much is given. Christians in the markets need to take special note.

However, it is not just the money that provides

opportunities. For, as noted already, retirement horizons are markedly shorter in the markets than in the economy as a whole. It might at first glance seem inconsistent with all that has been said above about finding God's purpose in our work life if we now begin to consider the implications of a short retirement horizon, but it is not. To do so is simply to recognize that our career need not – indeed, should not – be all there is to a life of Christian service. It also recognizes the circumstances of modern life (in which the world of the markets may well be something of a pathfinder for a more widespread tendency). More and more people need to take early retirement into account as a possible, or even probable, fact of life.

It is easy to overlook what a significant change this is. For most of history people worked until they dropped. In much of the world this is still true. Even in developed economies, the expectation has been that people work until well into their sixties, and life expectancy (at least for males) until relatively recently has been no more than about seventy. The expectation of a younger (and perhaps financially more secure) retirement than previous generations could have dreamed of, together with a life expectancy creeping up towards eighty, is spreading in our present generation. For people to retire in their early fifties, with perhaps twenty years of active life ahead of them, is now no longer uncommon.

This is by no means all of the story, of course. Often, early retirement is involuntary, and accompanied by great personal trauma. In any case, the prospects of a more affluent and financially secure retirement have by-passed large numbers of people, creating new divisions between the haves and the have-nots of society. Moreover, the rising cost of care for a longer-living population of elderly people will place new financial burdens on the working population. Modern Britain is nowhere near becoming a Garden of Eden. But the fact remains that growing numbers of people do find themselves in the position of being able to – or having to – retire early. Christians who do so need to take stock of the *opportunities* it represents, rather than just being mesmerized (however understandably) by the uncertainty of it all.

This will not, typically, be an easy process. Indeed, it can be a disturbing time for anyone. Not for nothing do we talk of the reappraisal which often takes place in peoples' forties and fifties as a mid-life crisis. The stories of those who joined their employing institution many years ago and fully expected to spend all their working life until a normal, fully pensioned retirement there, only to find themselves being made redundant or retired early, are now common. Many – including Christians – will testify to the disorientation and the loss of self-esteem that this experience can provoke. Since few Christians are 'super saints', it would be dishonest to deny the fear that often accompanies it all: the fear of inadequate provision for old age, or – more immediate – of being unable to maintain our existing home and living standard. Even for those without financial worries, there is often a gnawing sense of rejection and of failure, together with an unspoken and perhaps unconscious fear of having nothing to do.

For a Christian to face this as an opportunity, and not just as a threat, requires courage and trust. It requires a whole new search for a calling. What am I called to do *now*? This requires, as it did the first time round, prayer and Christian counsel, together with wisdom (to assess: what are my gifts? what skills do I have and could I realistically acquire? what, realistically, is my financial position? and so on). Christian churches are missing an exciting opportunity by not paying more attention to those reaching a time when it may be right to move on from their existing career and search for new possibilities. It is a time when new potential for Christian service can open up, and new life can begin.

Finally, we noted earlier that Christians could be called to sacrifice their career because of the requirements of integrity. But there is also another, entirely different, reason why we might be called to sacrifice our career – one which is perhaps in practice more likely to occur. God, who called us into our career at one stage, may call us out of it at another. He may use the opportunity of early retirement; he may even use the trauma of involuntary redundancy. He may also do so without either of these 'external' triggers: God may simply call us to something radically different. The evidence is that this happens to people in the most unexpected ways, and Christians have to recognize that no plans, no 'common sense' can be entirely proof against it. We have built up an understanding of God's dealings with humanity on the basis of a long tradition of people who have felt called by God out of the familiar into the unfamiliar. From Abraham, who is called out in his old age to a new country to found a new people; through to those early followers of Jesus who were called out of familiar occupations into the unpredictable role of itinerant disciple; through countless others down to the present day, people from all sorts of backgrounds have felt the call to sacrifice the known for the unknown.

Once again, the key is the calling. Beyond that, there may be no pattern – except for prayer, and probably the wisdom of others in the testing of our sense of vocation. All we can say is that it may happen and we should be prepared for it as a possibility. Our career – even if we are satisfied that we are called to it and relish it, seeing the potential for Christian service within it – is never an ultimate commitment. It may be overridden. We may be required to sacrifice it all. That is the point of Jesus' wisdom about the lilies of the field and the birds of the air: sit loose with it all, because you may be required to lose it all.

Conclusion

Christians can serve God in the world of finance and commerce, but it is also possible to fall into the trap of serving Mammon there. Yet the kingdom of God can be found in the thick of the markets and God calls some Christians to take the risk of being there. This does indeed involve risk – the risk of becoming compromised, of becoming obsessed with wealth and power, of selling one's soul. But the markets – flawed though they are, like every other human structure – can be used to contribute to human development. Being there also creates opportunities: to show an integrity that loves others as ourselves and treats them as ends rather than means; and to use the resources we are given as effective stewards should. In other words, we are there as Christians with a purpose.

The choice we should make is not Faust's choice – to sell our souls for gain – but what might be called Joshua's choice – the choice to serve God in the place to which we are called. In the words of the challenge he issues to his followers as they settle in the Promised Land:

> *Now, therefore, revere the Lord, and serve*
> *him in sincerity and faithfulness; put away*
> *the gods that your ancestors served*
> *beyond the River and in Egypt, and serve*
> *the Lord. And if you are unwilling to serve*
> *the Lord, choose this day whom you will*
> *serve, whether the gods your ancestors*
> *served ... or the gods of the land you are*
> *now living in; but as for me and my*
> *household, we will serve the Lord.*
> (Joshua 24:14–15)

But the last word belongs to that other Joshua, or – to use the Greek version of his name by which the New Testament knows him – Jesus. For he reminds us again that there is a choice:

> *No one can serve two masters; for a servant*
> *will either hate the one and love the other,*
> *or be devoted to the one and despise the*
> *other. You cannot serve God and Mammon.*
> (Matthew 6:24)